HIS RULE
IN HIS CHURCH

by Carlton Kenney

Distributed by:

MorningStar
PUBLICATIONS
P.O. Box 369 • Pineville, NC 28134

Table of Contents

FOREWORD

I have never read a book in which I have fully agreed with everything that was in it (including my own books when I reread them after a couple of years). I cannot say that I agree with everything that Carlton has written in this book, but I can honestly say that I agree with it more than just about any book that I have ever read. I am sure that I agree with it more than any book I have read on the subject of Church Structure and Authority.

Carlton is a revolutionary. Tempered by his long service as a missionary to one of the most difficult mission fields, Japan, he is gentle, patient, entreatable, genuinely humble, and one of the wisest men I have ever met. With his teachings or writings, you never feel pressured by dogma, but rather compelled by wisdom. Carlton's wisdom is not just a mental brilliance; it is derived from decades of searching the Scriptures, guided by a deep and sincere love of the truth.

Even so, Carlton is a revolutionary. His insights are radical and they will bring transformation—but not with a reactionary spirit. Those who simply love the truth and are not trying to protect a position or domain can afford to be gentle, patient, entreatable and they will always be humble. Those who love the truth search the Scriptures because of this love; and that love prohibits one from searching just to prove a point or verify a predetermined position. In Carlton's writings you do not feel like you're getting a pressured defense of a position—you feel like you're getting *discoveries*—treasures that have been mined, then shaped and polished.

As important as I believe some of the insights contained in this book may prove to be, I trust that you will also receive what I always receive from my times with Carlton—a sincere love of the truth.

Rick Joyner

INTRODUCTION

Thirty years ago one word was implanted in my heart that has germinated and continued to grow during the intervening years. It is from Moses' experience before building the Tabernacle. **"See that you make all things according to the pattern which was shown you on the mountain"** (Hebrews 8:5) *God has a pattern for His church*—how that word has impacted me! At that time I could not imagine any particular sense of stewardship in receiving a message like that. It was certainly gratifying to me personally as part of my quest for God, and being on the threshold of a missionary career to Japan, I thought that perhaps it was part of my preparation for that work.

In retrospect, I marvel at those early years in Japan. Japan has consistently been one of the difficult nations for the gospel. The official statistic — less than one percent Christian — has basically not changed. Churches are small. Why would the Holy Spirit exercise my mind with ideas about church structure and related concepts when the greatest need was evangelism? That little Japanese flock of about thirty saints was so patient to listen to this visionary share week after week his ideas about the pattern for the church and the way it was governed. That is not to say that other subjects were not ministered to them. I am grateful that I had enough sanity to share *some* things that were relevant to them in their walk with the Lord at that time!

During those years there were opportunities to visit the States. It was stimulating to compare my ideas with what I saw happening in the U.S. church. The Charismatic Renewal eventually made inroads into Japan, but it never reached the proportions it did in the States. More was happening in the U.S. and it fostered hope in me that a restoration of sorts was in progress. It was exciting to see things that had been visualized actually being birthed into experience. Among the churches I knew, I was permitted to see on a small scale a gradual implementation of some of the concepts. Even so, there was still much to be desired in the way of restoration.

In this book I attempt to examine the ways of church government. Whenever dealing with a study like this which majors on principles, I always feel an apprehension. I must voice a caution in two areas. First of all, a mechanical application of principles — regardless of how true they are — will not yield the desired results. There is no substitute for waiting upon God. The work of the Lord must be birthed out of communion with Him. The principles, at best, are guidelines. And secondly, we must make allowance for variations in the applications. I am firmly convinced that principles describe the ways of the Lord—ways which are foundational and do not change from generation to generation or from one culture to another. It is important to clearly define them. But in the application, we must make allowance for variations. Our God is a God of variety.

Finally, I must say something about my posture in presenting this subject. Back in the beginning when the message of God's order for the church was first presented to me, there was also a clarion call for God's people to "come out of Babylon." What that meant was that denominations and institutional forms of Christianity were not operating according to "the pattern." This meant that God's people should "come out" and be a part of forming a New Testament church. I could readily accept that it was His will for some to do that. I am numbered among those adventurous souls who wanted to be a part of such a church. However, I found it difficult to believe in that hour that God was setting the stage for a mass exodus. Where were the "Moses" or "Joshuas" who could lead such a movement? I just could not accept that to "come out" was a mandate of the Spirit for the entire Church in that hour.

Also, those who were national leaders in that hour were not defining it in terms of restoration. It was a renewal. We were told that God's purpose was not to alter existing denominations in their form but rather to revitalize its members. Some did not agree and in one way or another contended for restoration, but by and large "renewal" has been the climate of the Charismatic Movement. Some have felt that God *did* have a higher purpose and that He made it known in the late '40s and early '50s. It has even been intimated that influential men intentionally made concessions and guided the movement into the course it has taken. I do not feel qualified to address that. Eternity will reveal the truth. In any case, who was I as a young man to say otherwise? Consequently, because of my apprehension of a mass exodus and because of what national leaders were saying, I could not join whole-heartily with those who categorically said to the Body to "come out."

My stance for these thirty years has been to be still concerning the matter of coming out. Not because I do not cherish the hope for something like that to happen; I have dreamed my dreams. Instead, I have made it my aim to try to understand the pattern, to embrace tenaciously 'the heavenly vision.' To those who for one reason or another have come out, I have hoped that the books I have written could be of help in showing some alternatives for church life — alternatives which define the principles guiding the early church. And for those who are a part of a branch of Christianity which holds to different views of church life and *yet are victoriously walking with the Lord there,* I have never felt it my role to tell them to change that. God sets members in the church *as it pleases Him!*

It appears that the Charismatic Renewal has basically run its course and that the Church is being prepared for a new visitation. In a sense of soberness and fear of the Lord, I am constrained to reconsider my posture. I cannot say that God has commissioned me to contend with existing ecclesiastical systems or to issue an ultimatum to His people in those systems. But I can say that the time is coming when doing things according to God's ways will be a serious matter. The church is going to experience pressure in two ways. First, there will be external pressure. Too long the church in the West has escaped persecution. Ungodly forces are waiting to be unleashed upon us. It will test our mettle. And secondly, the Lord will surely arise in that hour to be with His people. There is going to be a new wine. That, too, will create a "pressure." It will be extremely difficult for stiff, unyielding wineskins to handle an intense visitation of the Spirit. God's ways, and His ways alone, are designed to handle those kinds of pressure.

Therefore, in sending forth this edition of *His Rule In His Church*, I am constrained to present it with a challenge. If we have treated lightly the matter of doing things according to God's ways, repentance may be in order. Each man must decide. First of all, contrition is important in our own relationship with the Lord Jesus Christ whom we claim to be our Sovereign. It is also important as a prerequisite for understanding the pattern. I conclude that from the way God dealt with Ezekiel about showing the pattern to Israel. Some things about the house they could understand just by his declaring it to them. Some they could not understand until they repented of their ways.

> **"As for you, son of man, describe the temple to the House of Israel, that they may be ashamed of their iniquities; and let them measure the plan. And if they are ashamed of all that they have done, make known to them the design of the house...and write**

it in their sight, so that they may observe its whole design and all its stature, and do them." (Ezekiel 43:10-11)

CHAPTER 1

THE MYSTERY OF LAWLESSNESS

"For the mystery of lawlessness is already at work. Only he who now restrains will do so until he is taken out of the way. And then that lawless one will be revealed..." (II Thessalonians 2:7-8)

In this generation we have certainly witnessed upheavals in society. Demonstrations, revolutions have been the order of the day. But let us not imagine that the Church is immune to these; we have had to contend with them within the body of Christ as well. I want us to think together about three forms by which lawlessness expresses itself to hinder the way Christ governs His Church. For convenience I refer to these as *anarchy, plurality, and usurpation.*

Anarchy simply means no government at all. We read of such a time in Israel's history: **"In those days there was no king in Israel. Every man did that which was right in his own eyes." (Judges 21:25)** Those today who are fed up with the establishment would likely find that as a positive commentary. With all the problems of bureaucracy and the various forms of government, would it not be advantageous to have more control in the hands of the people? Stated another way, would it not be better to have no government than to

1

have "bad" government? Not in the sight of God! The apostles teach us to respect civil government, notwithstanding its imperfections and irrespective of the particular form it takes.

This desire to be free of government in the church can be seen in one of the factions which existed at Corinth. Three of these groups were rallying around a leader (i.e. Paul, Apollos, and Cephas). The fourth group claimed to be "of Christ." In reality what these people meant is that they did not need *any* minister to lead them. They apparently felt that the Lord Himself would minister directly to them, and that was all they needed to be shepherded. However, it was this "of Christ" group that gave the apostle Paul the most difficulty (e.g. 2 Corinthians 10:7-10).

I think many saints today who model themselves after that fourth faction in Corinth are sincere in their ideals. It is not so much that they are deliberately setting themselves to resist the proper oversight. They feel that "uncontrolled" (and "unplanned") meetings are the way to attain liberty in the Spirit. Not only that, there are situations where God has really put His blessing upon those kind of gatherings. When there is no one to lead and saints come together seeking the Lord, He will meet with them. However, the test of their sincerity will come when the Lord Jesus begins to provide leadership for them. If anarchy is in their hearts, this "no-government-freedom-in-the-Spirit" way of doing things will stand up to resist what Christ is doing to bring in His normal procedure for governing the Church.

Co-equality is perhaps not as defiant as the first form of lawlessness, but is a problem nonetheless. Those in this group are championing the cause of plurality. This is misleading since teamwork is indeed the Lord's agenda. The Lord Jesus desires for leaders to work together in meaningful relationships! But often those in this camp are not merely contending for plurality; they expect this kind of eldership

2

to be without anyone among them leading in a prominent way. Thus, it is unlike anarchy inasmuch as there is an acknowledgement of men in governing roles. Nevertheless, plurality without headship is not the normal expression of His rule.

Sometimes churches are thrust into a situation where elders have to work co-equally. What about churches that lose their pastor and preparations have not been made for another to replace him? There is this interesting commentary about Israel:

"And Israel served the Lord all the days of Joshua, and all the days of the elders that outlived Joshua, and which had known all the works of the Lord, that He had done for Israel." (Joshua 24:31)

When a church is suddenly without its "Joshua," the Chief Shepherd's grace is upon them for a season. However, when the Lord Jesus begins to move to provide someone as lead-man for these elders and they resist it in preference for maintaining co-equality, we realize that another form of lawlessness is at work there.

What is *usurpation?* To the Ephesian elders Paul said,

"I know this, that after my departing shall grievous wolves enter in among you, not sparing the flock. Also, of your ownselves shall men arise, speaking perverse things, to draw away disciples after them." (Acts 20:29-30).

The two forms of lawlessness mentioned above deal with wrong concepts about church order, but this problem is different. The problem here is not wrong concepts, but wrong people — those who are not qualified getting into places of leadership. Those who lead the Church must qualify for that work! Indeed, if the enemy cannot prevent us from finding the right form and ways for church government, then he resorts to getting the wrong men into those positions.

Thus, anarchy, co-equality, and usurpation are the three forms of lawlessness I see which are making inroads into the church today. As we progress into the study, I will attempt to relate the teaching to these three forms of lawlessness. Thus, having described the problem, let us proceed to consider the solution.

CHAPTER 2

THE DIACONATE

The way Christ governs the church is through two leadership roles. The concept of these two is summed up in the Greek words: "diakonos" and "episkopos." For simplicity I have chosen to discuss them by their English transliteration: *diaconate and episcopate.* Much attention will be given to developing the idea of these two roles in the following pages. Let us first look at diaconate.

The most basic meaning of diaconate is "to serve." In many cases it means to serve with the hands. The English word "deacon" is taken from this word. In other cases it means to serve in a role of speaking the word of God. The way I will use diaconate is this second way — to single out those who are set apart as leaders in the Church. However, it is good from the outset to remind ourselves of the importance of leaders being humble of heart. By His life our Lord amply demonstrated this to those first apostles (Luke 22:24-27; John 13:1-17). We do not want to ever envision a leadership that is devoid of that humble, serving spirit!

After the day of Pentecost when the revival was at its peak, those apostles felt a great weight of responsibility. They had not forgotten the lessons of the Upper Room. It was a matter of priority. The time had come to appoint the first deacons (Acts 6:1-6). In response to the news of the problem Peter says, "It is not desirable for us to neglect the word of God in order to *serve* tables." With the appointment of deacons to meet that need he explains that "we will devote ourselves to prayer and the *ministry* of the word." Here two kinds of diaconate are mentioned: to serve tables and to serve in the Word. In this study we are considering diaconate in the more restricted sense that Peter describes their role as ministers of Christ. (The following are a list a Scriptures where diaconate is mentioned and usually translated as ministry: Acts 1:17, 25; 20:24; 21:19; Romans 11:13; II Corinthians 4:1; 6:3; Colossians 4:17; I Timothy 1:12; II Timothy 4:5).

Ephesians 4:11 is where the diaconate is listed: **"And He gave some as apostles, and some as prophets, and some as evangelists, and some as pastors and teachers."** I believe that this is a comprehensive and unique tally. First, there are five, and only five, basic styles in which the word of Christ is ministered. There can, of course, be variations of these and men may possess more than one of them (see I Timothy 2:7; II Timothy 1:11). But the list should not be appended with the other forms of "ministry" (e.g. elders, helps, governments, etc.).

Second, they are listed because of their common characteristics. For one thing, these are given within a particular time frame—from the ascension of Christ until the Body reaches its goal. For example, there was a special class of apostles prior to the Ascension who had things characteristic of their office which are not in common with the apostles and other four ministries listed here. Likewise, though we can say that there are similarities, we cannot say the Old Testament prophets and the ones listed here are exactly the same office. Another thing is the emphasis upon their gifting to speak the Word. It is in this restricted sense that we are to understand the role of *all five of these* in governing the church. We will see the importance of this when we begin to compare it with the episcopate. And thirdly, Paul does not intend for there to be any rank or order concerning these roles. In other listings rank is intended (I Corinthians 12:28), but here we are to understand that all five of these are equally necessary for the equipping of the saints.

To understand the nature of these five offices, we need to look at them in the context of Ephesians 4:7-16. It seems to me that Paul is not just giving us another teaching concerning a many-membered body with multiple giftings like he describes it in the Corinthian passage (I Corinthians 12:12-27). In that description "mouth" is just one of many functions. Peter suggests two basic roles for believers: Those who "serve" (without any particular function as "speakers" — and those who "speak" (I Peter 4:11). However, in the Ephesian passage the one phrase which describes the function of all the parts is "speaking the truth." It is a many-membered body where all have an anointing to speak the Word of God.

It is especially in this sense that we are to understand the equipping role of those five offices. This does not mean that the five-fold ministry are not concerned with the believers growing in character and all aspects of the Christian life. Indeed, the supply of all the parts is done "in love." It is futile to talk about an anointed church that does not demonstrate the fruit of the Spirit. But on the other hand, a church that does not have a rich deposit of all five of those anointings distributed among the members will come short of the fullness Paul speaks of, regardless of how mature it may be in character. With this setting in mind, let us look at the way that the Ascended Christ makes distributions in His Body. Two ways are mentioned.

The gifts are given to the men (v.8). This aspect of the Lord's distribution is not unique to those in leadership roles. It describes the way He deals with each member of the Body. Our focus here is to describe those in the classification of verse eleven. So, to say that the gifts are given to them means first of all that it is not a giftedness that is determined or defined by an immediate need. For example, if through prophecy or some other means the Holy Spirit were to single out a young man in the congregation as "a pastor," it would not necessarily mean that congregation is presently in need of a pastor. Rather, we would understand this to refer to a call of God to preach the gospel in that capacity—a calling which precedes in time the immediate situation (Jeremiah 1:5; Galatians 1:15). There is a process whereby that called-one comes into understanding of this and begins to cooperate with the realization of it in his life. Moreover, the Lord has so ordered the process that it is a direct transaction between Him and them. It is normal for the process to be assisted by the recognition and confirmation of others, but it is not absolutely essential to the process (Luke 3:2) Rather, because of this singular arrangement, the Lord can hold him personally accountable for the stewardship of the gift (I Corinthians 9:16-17; Colossians 4:17). In other words, these called-ones are personally in possession of the gift. This does not mean that the *manifestation* of the gift is not related to the immediate situation. Indeed, the response of people effects the expression of the gift (Matthew 10:41; Hebrews 5:11). Nevertheless, the gift is residual in those who have received it.

It also means that this giftedness is not determined or defined by relationships to particular groups of people. There is a restricted sense in which we can think of some leaders as "belonging" to particular parts of the Body of Christ. For example, we may refer to a certain minister as being "their" pastor. Or, in the case of apostle, Paul speaks of the sense in which his apostleship did not apply everywhere, but it did apply to the Corinthian church (I Corinthians 9:2) He was "their" apostle. Moreover, there is a sense in which there are shared anointings. The anointing the 70 elders experienced did not come directly from God, but was transferred from Moses' anointings. Paul was gracious in his epistles to use an editorial "we" referring to all the members of his apostolic team, but that does not mean that every brother was in fact an apostle (I Thessalonians 2:6). In other words, we must understand this distribution in the aspect of it being distinct from the way some ministers serve a particular part of the church (through developed relationships) and the way men work together in team relationships. Each of the Ephesians 4:11 offices are given to those men, and they possess it in a singular way.

The second way Christ makes distribution is by giving the men to the Church (v. 11). This describes the sphere of their responsibility. Each church is a sphere for the life and growth of the Body described in Ephesians four to transpire. But in the bigger picture these men are "given" trans-locally. Paul challenges the Corinthians about forming factions by rallying around a particular ministry to the exclusion of the other ministry. He reminds them that all are "theirs" (I Corinthians 3:21-23). Indeed, any leader who is in the Ephesians 4:11 classification has a commission which is trans-local or extra-local. We will see the importance of this when we begin to describe the governmental aspect of these offices.

In the sense of men being given to the church, we cannot include all believers in this operation. Within the sphere of the local church there is great opportunity for saints to develop in their anointings. But much consideration should be given to the prospect of them stepping out of that sphere. We see this in the careful steps taken by the church at Antioch to set apart the first two missionaries. When they put their blessing upon them, I believe that they were acknowledging at least three things about them.

First, they acknowledged that these two were in that role by virtue of a definite call of God — a call which is for life (e.g. "irrevocable" Romans 11:29). It is not a role which occupies them for a few years of their youth, or until they are married. Nor is it enough that they have an outstanding testimony and an anointing to match it; it is more precise than that. Secondly, at the time the church is recognizing them in this fashion, it is declaring that these men have attained a certain maturity in character and giftedness that makes it appropriate for them to operate trans-locally (Acts 15:22-27) And thirdly, they are recognizing that it is seemly for these men to receive their livelihood through the preaching of the gospel.

As the Charismatic renewal progressed there was an emphasis which resulted in believers being mobilized for ministry like we have not seen before. This was certainly the focus of the Holy Spirit. During this trend a number of para-church groups and other organizations emerged. Businessmen found an effective way to serve the Lord. Youth realized greater opportunities to be involved. And in all of this there was a gradual shift away from the idea of a special ministerial class and a tendency to remove any distinction between those in the Ephesians 4:11 category and the rest of the Body. The problem became manifest over a period of time when these mobilized believers operated outside the local church sphere. It is time for the pendulum to swing back the other way and for us to rediscover what the early church understood about these offices being given to the Body at large. We must see them in the context of this many-membered anointed Body as those set apart in a distinct way with an equipping role. And included in that role is a certain expression of government for the Church.

CHAPTER 3

THE EPISCOPATE

The basic meaning of "episkopos" is "to look diligently" (Hebrews 12:15). It also means "visitation" (Luke 19:44; I Peter 2:12). The word is translated as "oversight" or "bishopric" and the person in that role is a "bishop." Thus, an overseer is not merely one who is well acquainted with the situation (e.g. "to visit"). Another word which relates to this role is "heigeomai" which simply means "to rule" (Acts 15:22; Hebrews 13:7, 17, 24). And then there is "Proisteimi" which means "to stand before" (Romans 12:8; I Thessalonians 5:12; I Timothy 3:4; 5:17). It would be convenient if there was a single passage (like Ephesians four) where we have a concise listing or description of the role of overseers, but unfortunately that is not the case. Consequently we must study words such as I have just listed and form our definition.

Peter refers to God as the Shepherd and Overseer of our souls (I Peter 2:25). As we progress in our study we will see that these are complementary concepts. (e.g. shepherds are overseers and overseers shepherds.) In one translation the word for overseer in I Peter 2:25 is "guardian." That certainly suggests a special kind of responsibility for certain ones. The writer of Hebrews impresses upon us the serious sense of responsibility that these leaders feel in giving account to the Chief Shepherd for their oversight (Hebrews. 13:7). And

Peter tells the elders that the particular sheep they are responsible for are the ones "allotted to your charge." (I Peter 5:4). As we consider these ideas we realize that something other than five-fold ministry is being described.

Unlike the diaconate, the role of episcopate can only be described in terms of relationships to particular groups of people. Moreover, those relationships are developed and maintained by certain principles or functions which depict this work. We will examine those later. The important thing here is to make a distinction between the two roles. This is especially true in the case of those who are in both roles. For example, a man may be *the* pastor of a particular congregation, but when invited to speak to another congregation he would not be *their* pastor. In reality as far as Ephesians 4:11 is concerned he may be *a* pastor. That would mean that in both congregations his style for preaching would be the same (e.g. pastoral), but in government he would not relate the same. Moreover, it is possible that in the church where he is *the* pastor in reality as far as diaconate is concerned, he is a teacher or one of the other offices, but not a pastor! We will see as we progress in our study how this can be so. So let us now consider the various levels of administration in which episcopate is expressed.

The basic level is the local church. At the climax of their first missionary journey Paul and Barnabas ordained elders. They did this in *every* church (Acts 14:23). This is an important goal in church planting. When this goal is attained, that church has come into a kind of autonomy, the overseers there are called "elders." Some of these men may be faithful brothers who are not in the Ephesians 4:11 category. Others may be in that category. In either case, if they are indeed the episcopate, it is because they have given themselves to the functions describing that role and have been made so by the Holy Spirit (Acts 20:28).

Besides the local church, there are extra-local levels of oversight. The most obvious is that of an apostle as illustrated in the life of Paul. To the Corinthians he said, "If to others I am not an apostle, at least I am to you…" "To you" means more than simply to their way of thinking. He is describing the special relationship he has with them. The interesting thing is that there is no precise word (such as "elder") to describe his shepherding role toward them. In saying this, Paul is not denying his diaconate. Certainly he was one "given" trans-locally as an apostle and would be so anywhere he went. But concerning episcopate on an extra-local level of administration, he could only claim that with churches where the relationship existed. And he had no other way of identifying that particular aspect of his leadership except as part of his apostleship.

Another level of administration is intermediate to the local church and the administration of apostles. This is illustrated in the roles of two brothers — Timothy whom Paul sent to Ephesus and Titus whom he left in Crete. When we read the three pastoral letters written to these men we realize that they were not there simply in the role of a traveling ministry, but had received a charge from Paul. They were, so to speak, an extension of his oversight towards those particular churches. For convenience I refer to this level according to the traditional idea of "bishop." Yet, bishop is only another translation of "episkopos." Once again we are groping for a word. There is no precise word to uniquely describe this level of administration. Certainly as far as ministry is concerned, those men were in the Ephesians 4:11 category — probably emerging apostles. But for the shepherding role they had to those particular churches, there is no biblical title for it. Thus, we have three levels of administration where overseeing might possibly be expressed.

Let us conclude this chapter by summarizing a few of the differences between those in the role of the five-fold ministry and those who are overseers:

1. **Diaconate**: These leaders are given trans-locally and "belong" to the entire Body of Christ.

   Episcopate: These leaders realize their role only in the sphere where special relationships are developed with particular groups of sheep.

2. **Diaconate:** There are descriptive words to describe each of these offices.

   Episcopate: Except in the local church level of administration, there are no descriptive words to precisely describe these shepherding roles.

CHAPTER 4

THE WORK

"It is a trustworthy statement: if any man aspires to the office of overseer, it is a fine work he desires to do" (I Timothy 3:1).

From these words of Paul we want to further develop the concept of the episcopate. The overseers Paul has in mind here are in the local church — elders. We need first of all to specify which elders these are. The New Testament practice of establishing or recognizing elders is derived from Israel's national tradition, which is taken from the instructions of the Lord to Moses when he cried out to God for help for discharging his oversight role:

"Gather for Me seventy men from the elders of Israel, whom you know to be the elders of the people and their officers and bring them to the tent of meeting, and let them take their stand there with you" (Numbers 11:16).

Moses is instructed to choose elders from a body of elders already in existence. I will mention briefly here the differences of these two types of eldership. Let us look at this already existing body of elders whom I refer to as *general elders.*

These are the older men of the nation who have walked with God a number of years. "The hoary head is a crown of

15

glory and is exalted in the way of righteousness" (Proverbs 16:31 Lamsa Translation). They are "exalted in the way" as elders by their own testimony. That means first of all, that this is not an appointed position, but one they have "earned" with the people. And secondly, by the very nature of gaining such credibility, the emphasis is upon age; it takes time to establish a testimony! Moreover, God does not seem to set limits upon that kind of eldership. When God spoke those words to Moses, there were hundreds of these elders in Israel! How do these elders exert their influence in a congregation?

Basically, they are like pillars in the church. Just their presence gives a sense of security and stability. They can even be considered as counsellors in a limited sense. It is natural that younger believers will gravitate to them and want to open their hearts for instruction. These men can in a general way teach them the ways of the Lord. They have much to offer from their wisdom and experience. And up to a certain point they can give direction to these sheep seeking their help. However, if these men are not a part of the official eldership and they attempt to guide these sheep in specific areas of decision for their lives, there will be problems. There will be a conflict with the normal shepherding process through the appointed elders of the church. Thus, it is valuable to a church when these men are allowed to have their influence in the congregation. But the workability of this depends upon their acknowledging the limitations of their influence and their continually exercising restraint along these lines.

The other group of elders I call *governing elders or official elders*. They are appointed to this position. It is important to realize that we are talking about a distinctly different group, now. Those general elders, even though they have in one sense been accepted by the congregation—they do not automatically and necessarily come into this official eldership.

Moses had to pass over many qualified elders in order to limit his selection to only seventy. On the other hand, governing elders are not necessarily the oldest ones. Paul stipulates that they must not be novices, but he does not define exactly what that is (1 Timothy 3:6). There certainly must be some approval of these men. They cannot be too young, but how young? The elders Paul and Barnabas appointed on their first trip were saved at the same time as the rest of the congregation—a matter of months! Nevertheless, since this kind come about by appointments and not like the first group gaining their acceptance entirely by their testimony, this no-novice requirement can be interpreted relative to the needs of that congregation. It makes a difference when "young" overseers are appointed by older leaders who are standing with them in that role (1 Timothy 4:12; Titus 2:15).

In this trustworthy statement Paul makes about overseers, he has to be talking about this second group. He is giving guidelines to Timothy for making appointments. It is needless for Paul to discuss that about general elders. Those elders, in a sense, "appoint" themselves by virtue of their testimony and they remove themselves when they do things to destroy their credibility with the people. The elders Paul is considering are the group who "rule" ("direct the affairs of the church" NIV I Timothy 5:17). It is these governing elders who are the episcopate of the local church. Exactly what is this "work" for which these men are being appointed?

In this passage we have the phrase "office of overseer", when in reality "office" does not occur in the original. This phrase is just one word which simply means "bishopric" or "overseership". It would be a mistake for us to envision this "office" as a position in a hierarchy. I think one of the great mistakes in church history was for people to fail to recognize the changing nature of the episcopate. What was in the first generation a vibrant system of relationships between overseers and sheep a few generations later degenerated into a rigid and stagnant hierarchy. Writings during the period right after the apostolic era often use phrases such as "episcopal office" or even "episcopal seat". How strong is the tendency of the church to make her ecclesiastical systems! It is important that an assessment is made periodically and adjustments made in the "system" to agree with the reality of what Christ is doing to govern the work. How are we to understand this "reality"?

Paul refers to this role as being a fine work. Work means there is in reality a job that needs to be done. When Moses cried to God for help it was because the workload was too much for one man. God responded to *a need Moses felt*. God did not take the initiative and impose upon Moses a group of men that were not really needed. Likewise, Paul and Barnabas did not appoint elders as the initial phase of their visit in the work of church planting. They were the eldership at that point and did not feel a need for others until it was time for them to leave. There is the right time in a work for these things to happen, and when it does happen at that time, it is "beautiful" (Ecclesiastes 3:11). On the other hand, if we view this as something like a hierarchy with vacant "seats" or "offices" waiting to be filled and we proceed as soon as possible to fill these, it will be so artificial!

Another consideration regarding this workload is that when the right time comes, there are the right number of men to meet that need. God specified a certain number for Moses to choose. One of the reasons for this relates to the way eldership must work. The general elders do not affect the congregation as a group. Their role can be fulfilled as an individual senior member of the body. They do not need to coordinate with other elders as long as they are acting within the limitations previously mentioned. But governing eldership, by its very nature, requires that those men in that group be deeply involved in communicating and coordinating. To do this practically, it must be limited to a number which is functional. However, there is something yet even more basic to considering the right number.

The number of men should somewhat correspond to the size of the congregation. The reason for that is that normally the size of the congregation will determine the amount of work to be done. The number of elders must approximately correspond to the workload. I cannot think of anything more frustrating for a pastor and for his elders than to have more men than is realistically needed. Very often the reason this happens is there has not been clarity about the two kinds of eldership. Pastors feel guilty about not including all the qualified men. A more realistic course of action is to appoint only the men really needed and find a way to honor those general elders and allow them to have their input from time to time. *Eldership must be regarded as a work which needs to be done and not as a position for honoring the faithful men of the church!* Thus, "work" means not only that there is the right time for these things to happen, but that there is a correspondence of the work-load to the number of men being appointed.

Another thing which must be considered about these appointees for eldership is their availability for the "fine work". A man may be qualified in every way, but his schedule just would not allow him to give himself to it. I cannot stress too much that this is not a position for honoring men, but a job which needs to be done. There is no such thing as an inactive elder; it is a contradiction of words. A man on the eldership, for whatever reason may resign his place in the eldership. If the reasons are honorable, probably in the eyes of the people he will be regarded as a general elder. In that sense only he is an inactive elder, but why call it that? *All* general elders are in that category, not "actively" a part of the governing body. The same is true for those who move out of the area for an extended period of time. It is a misnomer to call them "elders-at-large". The sphere of their eldership can only be defined "at home". And when they are out of that sphere, there is no eldership to refer to. The empty "spot" in that team they are away from is not a position for them to retain during their absence or inactivity. We must think of overseeing as a "work" that needs to be done and the men being considered must be available to do it. What about extra-local levels of administration?

We mentioned the two examples of bishops. Is it not significant that Paul did not appoint bishops in all areas? Since he did not, I have to conclude that some of those areas did not need them. And what about apostles in oversight relationships to churches? Do all churches need this? Certainly all churches can profit from the *ministry* of apostles as well as all the Ephesians 4:11 offices. However, it is conceivable to me that churches can grow strong enough in their eldership that there is no need of oversight on a higher level. I think this would be true in the case where the senior pastor is himself as apostle (or an emerging apostle). One of the strongest churches in the New Testament was Antioch. It was not the fruit of apostolic labor, nor is there any intimation that anyone was overseeing it on a higher level of administration. Apostles are not mentioned until Paul and Barnabas are sent for their missionary endeavors. *This church "birthed" the apostles and not the other way around!*

When we think of the "fine work" that describes overseeing, we must assess both in the local church and extra-locally the reality of the need. In the local church uniquely we have a title to describe the men in those roles. Perhaps the Lord wants us to understand by this that there is something that is not-so-changing in the sphere of the local church. In other words, once the church in its history has reached the point of having elders ordained, it does not reach a future condition where it no longer needs elders. There will likely be change as to who those elders are, and as the church grows there will be need for additional elders, but never a condition where there will be no need for elders. However, it will not be so outside the sphere of the local church. On these higher levels of administration, the episcopate must adjust to the reality of what is needed.

Concerning bishops and shepherding apostles, we are not only saying that there are cases where those roles do not come into existence with some churches. There comes a time when there is no need to continue those roles. For example, consider the system of relationships Paul developed with churches. He directly related to a number of churches as an apostle in oversight. In at least two cases there was the intermediate role of bishops (Timothy and Titus). What was supposed to happen when the time came for him to pass off the scene? Are those relationships between overseer and churches to be regarded as a hierarchy with offices or episcopal seats that are to exist in perpetuity? *There is no hint that Paul was expecting someone to be his successor* in that sense. Indeed, when an overseer passes off the scene, it is not always a case of a vacancy that is waiting to be filled. It is time to reassess that episcopate with the possibility that there is no need to continue it. If the need does not exist, then there is no justification for that episcopate to be perpetuated!

Let us consider the way the Lord draws men to these roles of responsibility. When we discussed diaconate, we saw that the way God draws men into those roles is by a call. Those men are *called to preach the gospel*. Men with that call feel a sense of "compulsion", a sense of direct accountability to God. It is not unjust for the Lord to hold them accountable inasmuch as it is fully within the realm of their own personal choice to discharge that call. It is a direct arrangement between them and God. Of course, it assists the process for there to be the confirmation of others, and even the tutoring of others, but it is not absolutely essential. The Bible abounds with examples of messengers of God who excelled in their mission solely by their own submission to the grace God offered them. But what about the episcopate? Is it appropriate for men to say they are called to be elders?

Paul did not put it in those terms. He refers to men having a "desire". That does not make it a small matter. We are warned to be careful in making our plans because God works in our heart by putting desires there (Philippians 2:12-13). Nevertheless, I think there is good reason to speak of men being drawn into this by a "desire" rather the a "call". Fulfilling these aspirations is not possible by a direct arrangement between those aspirants and God. These instructions were given to Timothy who was in a position to appoint them. But Paul is not promising that the desire is a guarantee of the fulfillment. It should be apparent by now that unlike the five-fold ministry, overseeing is a work defined and determined by many variables. It is limited in number. The need for it changes which means there can be situations where it is not needed anymore. If an elder moved to another city, he would not take his eldership with him in the same sense that ministers possess their gifts. It would be frustrating for men to think of it like a call—feeling a sense of accountability like five-fold ministry—and yet be dependent upon so many conditions being met *that they cannot directly effect*. Let us rather regard the episcopate as something into which God draws us with a preparation of heart by a desire. And having been placed into that role, by the Holy Spirit, it is like a "stewardship" (Titus 1:7). There is definitely a sense of responsibility for those sheep allotted to their charge *for as long as that stewardship lasts*. Yet, that is different from the calls of God which are for life and to be regarded as irrevocable.

Let us summarize this chapter by adding two more observations to the things listed at the end of the previous chapter:

1. **Diaconate**: These leaders have a calling and gifts which are irrevocable. They possess this in a way which is not dependent upon the context of their ministry.

   Episcopate: These leaders have this role only as long as it is maintained with those particular groups.

2. **Diaconate**: The calling to ministry is not to be regarded as a seasonal thing, but a life-time responsibility.

   Episcopate: Overseeing is not a position or office fixed by an ecclesiastical hierarchy. Rather, it is a stewardship defined and determined by many variables. It can only be developed where the need for it legitimately exists. It is to be perpetuated only as long as that need continues to exist.

CHAPTER 5

THE MEASURE OF THE GIFT

In the previous three chapters we described the two different roles of leadership through whom Christ expresses government to the Church. Now let us begin to describe the actual dynamics of the development and expression of each of these roles. These can be defined by *The Measure of the Gift* which corresponds to the diaconate, and *The Measure of the Rule* which corresponds to the episcopate. In this chapter we will consider the diaconate by studying 1 Timothy 1:12. "And I thank Christ Jesus our Lord, who has enabled me, for that He counted me faithful, putting me into the ministry". This gives us a good outline to study. First of all, He "has enabled me"; secondly "counted me faithful"; and finally, "putting me into the ministry". Let us consider these three operations.

In Romans 1:5 Paul says that he had received "grace" and "apostleship". Apostleship describes the type of ministry, and grace is what makes the ministry work. In Ephesians 4:7 he says that it is grace according to the measure of the gift—the same two things expressed another way. That is, in Paul's case the measure of gifting which Christ apportioned him was apostleship. For the other offices, the measure of the gift is described by each of those descriptive words in Ephesians 4:11. This is something God decides. And it is something He makes known to those men by a definite call. It is presumptuous for us to take this work upon ourselves if we have not truly been called unto it (Hebrews 5:4).

Paul was very much aware that without the grace of God, that calling would never be realized. "For I am the least of the apostles...but by the grace of God I am what I am. And his grace which was bestowed upon me was not in vain, but I labored more than they all. Yet, not I, but the grace of God which was with me" (I Corinthians 15:9-10). And in another passage he describes this grace as "the effectual working of His power" (Ephesians 3:7). And again he describes it as a mighty energizing (Colossians 1:29). Indeed, from the earliest awareness of a call that grace is already given to help those servants seek the Lord and prepare themselves for that role. And that grace continues with them in the following years after preparation as the dynamic of that ministry.

The second part of this operation for fulfilling a ministry concerns man's responsibility. Paul said that God counted him faithful. We are not told specifically what areas the Master is testing His servants in, but I like to regard it in the three areas He mentions in one of His teachings on stewardship (Luke 16:1-13). Faithfulness in little things, faithfulness in natural things, and faithfulness in another man's things! Each of those three are loaded with meaning. Thus, God looks for faithfulness *before* He works with His servants to place them into ministry. And *after* they begin experiencing that grace, they must respond in diligence. Thus, without detracting from the marvel of that grace, Paul makes it clear that he cooperated. He said, "I labored more abundantly than they all," and also, "whereunto I also labor, striving according to His working..." (I Corinthians 15:9; Colossians 1:29). God truly gives grace, but His servants must respond in the obedience of faith.

Finally, the third step is the actual fulfillment when God places them into that role. Normally this begins on a small scale in ministerial opportunities within the local church. In Timothy's case doors opened for him to minister in two churches—Lystra and Iconium. And finally he was afforded opportunity to become a part of Paul's team and minister trans-locally (Acts 16:1-3). There are a variety of ways that this can happen, but in every case it should be a demonstration of the Lord working with His servants to open those doors. And when God does open those doors and His servants are prepared and enter in, it is beautiful to behold!

Concerning this third step, it will be helpful to discuss the way God brings a minister into specialization. It is interesting the way Paul summarized his ministry: a preacher, an apostle, and a teacher (II Timothy 1:11). "Apostle" and "teacher" we recognize as part of the Ephesians 4:11 list, but why "preacher"? Is not preaching inherently a part of those five ministries? Why list it distinctly like this? I want to make three observations about this.

First, when the Lord places men into ministry, it is unusual for them to be initially placed into a role defined so clearly by one of those five categories. Normally there is a gradual process while they are actively engaged in ministry whereby this kind of definition is realized. But until that time, there is an initial stage that is distinct and recognizable whereby we can know men are in the diaconate. This is termed simply "preacher". We have discussed that those in these diaconate roles are set apart in a distinct way from the rest of the Body. We are now saying that in the initial phase of their ministry when they are set apart, the measure of the gifts does not have to be clearly defined.

Secondly, this initial phase should be characterized by commitment to both a message and a process for delivering that message. They are preachers of the gospel. "Gospel" defines a definite message which the Lord has entrusted to the stewardship of the ministry, a message which we must be thoroughly acquainted with and which remains central in all our preaching and teaching. And "preaching" describes the process which God has ordained for proclaiming that message. Paul makes no apology for how foolish this process seems, but rather defends it as a powerful method for Christ to work through His servants (I Corinthians 1:21-24). The ministry must remain faithfully committed to both the message and the process. *Occasionally men become so deeply involved in administrative roles or other functions they neglect their preaching role. When that happens, an important calling is stifled.*

Thirdly, when ministers move into areas of specialization, or when they move into another office of ministry, they do not lose what they formerly operated in. When Paul moved into his apostolic role, he did not lose his gifting as a teacher. And even more important, when he began to function as a teacher, and later as an apostle, he still viewed himself as a preacher. Pastors may be tempted to relegate the gospel to the evangelistic office as their message. Or teachers may tend to see their role as only teaching and not preaching. That would be unfortunate! Something is lost when any of those Ephesians 4:11 leaders do not retain preaching the gospel as a basic expression of their ministry. May God's grace be richly upon these men and may He may grant them to move full orbit in what it means for them to be placed into ministry.

CHAPTER **6**

THE MEASURE OF THE RULE

"But we will not boast of things without our measure, but according to the measure of the rule which God has distributed to us, a measure to reach even unto you" (II Corinthians 10:13).

This word "rule" is "kanonos" in the original Greek. It is the word from which our English word "canon" is derived. It literally means a straight rod (e.g. "cane"). And by its usage it means a sphere of action or influence. The translation of this phrase in the Japanese Bible gives a more precise idea of this concept. It is a sphere of influence *which is limited*. Right away this alerts us that Paul is not referring to his diaconate. The sphere of his influence and the government expressed through his ministry would be limited only by his travels and his ability to "faint not" (II Corinthians 4:1-18). Moreover, he qualifies the extent of this rule by saying it is "a measure to reach *even unto you*" (implying that it does not reach everywhere). This has to refer to the work of overseeing. Thus, *measure of rule* is a concept which describes the way Christ expresses government through the episcopate.

In chapter three I mentioned various words relating to the idea of overseeing. From these words and from examples in the Acts, there are three distinct functions for those in roles of oversight. If the Lord truly is distributing a measure of rule through a leader so as to place him in the episcopate, it will happen through fulfilling these three functions. Not only will that oversight be developed through those three things, it must be maintained the same way. Let us consider these.

The first function I call *meaningful involvement*. When giving requirements for eldership, Paul equates *ruling* the household with *taking care* of the church (I Timothy 3:5). This word "take care" is the same one used in the Lord's parable to show how the good Samaritan got deeply involved in that poor man's life in order to help him. Peter charged the elders to oversee sheep which are "among" them (II Peter 5:1-4) or conversely, the sheep which they are among—the ones they are meaningfully involved with. I might mention here that some leaders seem to operate on the premise that it is God's plan for them to oversee every person that is touched by their ministry! How unrealistic to feel a responsibility like that! But on the other hand, if we *are* to oversee, it must be a functional arrangement. The overseer must be realistic about his availability logistically and time-wise.

It goes without saying that included in this meaning is a quality of the way it is fulfilled. In a day when there is a euphoria about church growth and talk about mega-churches, we need to remind ourselves of the Chief Shepherd's priorities. It can certainly be said that God's heart is towards the masses of needy humanity. We do not ever want to lose sight of that. Yet we see the Lord Jesus in His priestly prayer turning His focus from a needy world and concentrating on a few (John 17:9). The High and Lofty One who inhabits eternity, the One who takes heaven for His throne and the earth for a footstool just does not get impressed with mega anything. His eye is upon the individual—"to this *one* I will look" (Isaiah 66:1-2). One of the four rebukes about the unfaithful shepherd is that he will not go and strengthen the one sheep standing alone in the pasture (Zechariah 11:16). When Paul speaks to those aspiring to be overseers, he says the work they aspire to is "good" (I Timothy 3:1 KJV). Let us not think of this goodness in terms of bigness, but rather in terms of personalism.

The second function of overseeing in *watching*. Those who feel this responsibility for particular sheep are described thus: **"...they keep watch over your souls, as those who will give an account" (Hebrews 13:17).** Perhaps the writer of Hebrews addresses believers in general when he says "See to it (i.e. oversee) that no one comes short of the grace of God;..." In other words, there is a sense in which we all are our brothers keeper and should be watchful. However, to speak of some "as those who will give an account" appears to be singling out particular ones and distinguishing them with a greater weight of responsibility. Overseers must give themselves to prayer for those allotted to their care!

Closely related to this watchfulness is a special kind of concern or *travail*. When Paul heard of the legalism that crept into those first congregations in Galatia, he describes his concern simply as travailing again in birth for them (Galatians 4:19). Perhaps the pathos of such a statement evades our comprehension, but a serious consideration of his list of sufferings should alert us to the gravity of this work. After going through a list of over twenty kinds of sufferings, he concludes with **"Apart from such external things, there is the daily pressure upon me of concern for all the churches" (II Corinthians 11.28).** Can you imagine his comparing this travail with such things as thirty-nine lashes with the whip, or some of those privations? Truly, there is a price to pay to faithfully fulfill this charge.

The third function of overseeing is found in (II Thessalonians 5:12). This verse talks about those who are "over" us. Now, it is true that the ministry of Ephesians 4:11, those given to the Body trans-locally are in a general sense "over" the Church. We will discuss that later. But I think this verse is referring to the more specific way in which some are "over" others in the kingdom of God. When Peter addresses the elders, he does not tell them to *not* be "over" those sheep, but *he warns them not to lord it over them.* It is good, therefore, for those with this responsibility to be of a humble mind and see themselves as postured "before" the ones they lead. But it is good for those being led to see these leaders as "over" them, and receive them in that manner. Thus, Paul is not soliciting appreciation for the ministry in general, but specifically for those who "have charge over you in the Lord *and give you instruction*". So, the third function of overseeing is *speaking the word of God.* Obviously the Ephesians 4:11 ministers speak the word of God to the church. Is there an essential difference in the way the diaconate speak it and the way the episcopate speak it?

I have already mentioned that overseeing and pastoring go together. It is interesting to me that the three times this verb form of pastor is used, two of them are instructions to overseers (Acts 20:28; I Peter 5:2). Feeding is not a term used to describe the quality of a minister's preaching. We may be impressed with the content of a gifted teacher's presentation, to say nothing of the clarity and inspirational way he gives it. When we think of his message "feeding" us, we usually are saying that he has given us something good, something important to think about. But if he has come as one given trans-locally, and is not one of our overseers, can we really call that "feeding"? By the very definition, feeding can only be done by those who are in a shepherding relationship with the ones receiving that instruction. To really understand the concept of feeding, we must first look in the Old Testament where the concept begins.

The civil leaders were referred to as shepherds (or "feeders") of Israel (II Samuel 5:2; I Chronicles 17:6; Psalm

78:71-72). In what manner did kings and judges "feed" Israel? Did they read the Law to the people? Where they instructors of the way of the Lord? Basically, this was not the case. Primarily the burden for instructing the nation fell upon the priesthood. The "feeding" of these kings and judges was something like this: They had the wisdom to discern between good and evil. They also had authority for their office. By this wisdom and authority they executed judgement by directing and watching over the spiritual food that the people partook of. They caused the people to walk by God's standard. They were those sent by God for the punishment of evildoers, and for the praise of them that do well (I Peter 2:14). In this manner they fed the people. How does this apply in the Church?

Those who oversee have a special burden for the people. They are concerned that the people walk according to godliness. They desire to see the teaching of God's Word applied to the lives of the sheep in a personal way. And these overseers themselves are involved with the sheep in a personal way. Consequently, their exhortations can be very direct and practical for those sheep. Timothy and Titus were overseers of particular churches. Paul told them to "reprove, rebuke, and exhort with all longsuffering and doctrine" (II Timothy 4:2; Titus 2:15). That well describes feeding.

In a local church a pastor is in a relationship with the people where he can feed them. Suppose that a teacher comes into their midst. As far as teaching or instructing is concerned, he may be capable of doing this with greater skill than the pastor. However, when it comes to the personal application of those things, who is better qualified that the pastor or elders for doing this? Likewise, a prophet is quite capable in preaching. The very style of his delivery of the Word is direct and searching. Even so, he is not in the same position as the ones in the episcopate when it comes to making personal application in the lives of the sheep. I realize

33

that there are exceptions to this. God can, and often has, raised up those who are "outsiders" (as far as episcopate is concerned) to come into a congregation and deliver the Word in specific ways. However, God's preferred way, the most seemly way for making *application* of the message is through the overseers.

To conclude the description of this function of overseeing, all of the five-fold ministry have an important role in speaking the Word of God to the Church. But "feeding" is a concept that describes the way overseers speak to the specific groups of sheep they are responsible for. These "feeders" have in mind moral standards and basic doctrines of the faith. And to a certain extent (through their involvement with those sheep) they know the Chief Shepherd's will for their lives. According to their understanding of that will, and according to the things they and the ministers of Christ have spoken, they guide the flock into right paths. They reprove and rebuke the unruly ones. They encourage and comfort the faithful ones. This is feeding.

Let us pause here and recap some of the things we have said. In chapter two we described what the five-fold ministry is and in chapter five we considered the dynamic of its operation. In chapter three and four I defined what overseeing is and in this chapter we looked at the three functions which describe the dynamics of it: meaningful involvement, watching with travail, and feeding sheep. To complete our picture of the episcopate, we need to take one more chapter and discuss the place of headship in the midst of plurality.

CHAPTER 7

A MAN

"And Moses spake unto the Lord saying, 'Let the Lord, the God of the spirits of all flesh, set a man over the congregation...that the congregation of the Lord be not as sheep which have no shepherd'" (Numbers 27:16-17).

Moses prayed for the Lord to supply *a* man, a man to be *the* shepherd of Israel. It was accepted at that time that it is reasonable for one man to be the shepherd of the nation. Yet, this concept is not so reasonable to some today who feel strongly that authority is given only to a *group* of men who are co-equal in ruling. To the credit of these people we must say that they are zealous to see ruling expressed through a group of men. This is to be appreciated inasmuch as teamwork is truly the Lord's agenda. But plurality operating with *co-equality* is not His way!

The main premise of their position is to argue from the "silence" of the New Testament. Because the New Testament does not give us detailed explanations concerning the governing of the churches, and because it speaks always of elders of the churches in plurality without clear reference to an individual among them who is the pastor, they assume that there is no one man who is the overseer. This is a strong assumption! Remember that such words as "elders, "feeding," and "shepherds" ("pastors") do not have their origins in the New Testament. These are concepts which begin in the Old Testament and have been brought over into the New where the apostles gave them application for the churches. We must study the original idea of these concepts. If we can establish that co-equality is indeed the way, then the "silence" concerning the single overseer in the New Testament can be construed as a confirmation of the original idea. On the other hand, if co-equality was not the way of things in the Old Testament economy, we should construe the "silence" to mean that nothing changed and *the principle is so obvious that the New Testament need not be explicit*. Indeed, if co-equality was not the way of Israel's economy, it is incumbent upon those who espouse this concept to bring forth plausible reasons for the change in the New Testament.

Looking at the Israel's history we realize that their first form of government was just after the exodus from Egypt. For a short while one man—Moses—was both the civil and religious head of the nation. However, soon afterwards the government was divided into a civil and a religious body. On the religious side there was the Aaronic priesthood with the high priest as *the one* in the highest level of authority. That body of government remained relatively the same in its form throughout the Old Testament era. However, on the civil side government went through various changes.

Moses was replaced by Joshua. He was a military leader for the nation who was supposed to coordinate his plans with the high priest (Numbers 27:21). From the scripture we first quoted we see that this successor of Moses was filling a need for Israel to not be as sheep without a shepherd. And after Joshua, the next form of civil government was the judges. After the period of the judges came the kings, of whom Saul was the first. This continued up until the Babylonian captivity. After the captivity the civil leaders of leaders of Israel were known as governors or "tirshatha". This form of government came into being when Israel became tributary to a foreign power. When she was a free nation, her leaders were either captains, judges, or kings.

Some have pointed out that in the change of the form of government from judges to kings, the Lord was displeased. The Lord said that Israel was rejecting Him as being their Sovereign (I Samuel 8:7). These proponents of co-equality have read too much significance into this displeasure. They interpret this to be a statement of Jehovah that "kingship" is not His form of government. Consequently, they feel that we cannot take any principles from this order of things as a pattern for us today. Can we really say that? At least we know from this incident that it was not the Lord's will for Israel to have a king *at that time*. Saul might have made a great judge, but the temptations of the king's office were apparently too much for him. As a nation Israel at that time was not ready for a king. But to say that Israel was to never have a king is to negate the prophecy of Jacob over his son Judah, that "the scepter shall not depart from Judah, nor the rulers staff from between his feet, until Shiloh (Jesus) comes" (Genesis 49:10).

The main point in all of this is that whether it be a judge, a king, or a governor, a basic principle still remains the same: *there is one with the final authority for ruling*. This is true both in the religious government as well as in the civil government. Obviously a judge is less of a monarch than a king. Nevertheless, he still has final authority in ruling. The principle remains constant throughout the Old Testament period though the form in which it is expressed changes. Also, whether it be Joshua as a military leader, or judges, or kings, all are referred to as those who "fed" Israel. They were shepherds! In Israel's society there were sub-levels of administrations to this one man shepherd. Those leaders may have been regarded as shepherds also, and they possibly operated somewhat co-equally. Even so, those sub-levels were not autonomous entities, but were ruled over by *the* shepherd.

If these concepts of "feed" and "shepherd" in the Old Testament have been consistently expressed with a lead-man overseer, should we not expect the Lord to tell us if there is to be a basic change in the pattern? Are we to visualize local churches as autonomous groups governed *only* by a body of elders who are co-equal in ruling? If this is the way shepherding *is* to be expressed, then we have a new form—a new way for which we have so little in the Scriptures to guide us. Rather than striving for a new principle (which really is not clearly proven) for feeding God's people, it is more reasonable for us to accept the one already given from the beginning and devote ourselves to learning the way it is to be expressed in the Church.

The formation of the government in the infant churches would have been a beautiful thing to behold. The apostles were not themselves "creating" the government for those assemblies, but rather were like midwives assisting the birth. Each assembly when "birthed" is a complete body. It is the body of Christ. And when born, is born with a head on it. Their role was to identify who were the men that constituted that headship. With a sense of awe, they did only the things that were expedient—nothing more. We know that they at least ordained the elders. What more they did than that would vary according to the need in each situation. If a need existed, I don't think they hesitated, by the direction of the Holy Spirit, to appoint one of those elders to be the coordinator for the whole assembly. If the need did not exist, they just left it with the ordination of the elders. As much as possible they allowed this lead-man to emerge from this body of elders by the anointing.

Let us recall what has already been said in chapter four about the changing nature of the episcopate. We can see this depicted in the Acts like various stages of development. The earliest stage is found in Acts fourteen where elders were appointed in every church. Probably at this stage of development the emergence of the lead-man was slow. On a higher level of administration there was strong apostolic ministry guiding those new churches. Because of this, at that stage of their development the need for *the* pastor was not so great. Later on, in some situations bishops were appointed. In that stage of development the apostle's own overseership was shifted more to bishops. And in those cases, because of the bishop's involvement, the need on the local church level for the leading overseer still would not be so great. However, eventually apostles like we see in the early church passed off the scene. In some parts of Christianity they retained bishops.

Many churches eventually became fully autonomous. In those cases, with none on a higher level of administration to oversee them, it was inevitable that the ministry of a "pastor" such as we have today would emerge. The need for a strong leader was very real. However, some today look at the strong leader type pastor and compare it with what is depicted in the earliest stages of apostolic church planting and say that it is all wrong. These fail to understand or acknowledge the changing nature of the episcopate, or they simply overreact to the stifling hierarchy of church government which later emerged.

In making a case for a lead-man to oversee in churches, I realize that it leads to many questions. Obviously that arrangement could create temptations for a man who is immature and sometimes not rightly motivated. If he is excessively "strong" and does not have a vision for Body ministry, he probably will not allow sufficient opportunity for "every joint to supply". He also may be reluctant to really make room for men to work alongside him in eldership. Or, if he does make room, those elders will likely become "yes men". Or, the pastor who is insecure will have his own struggles.

He will probably hold on too tightly to the reins. We must understand that the most perfect and Biblical form of church government can be corrupted by men with evil motives or unwise practices, but that is not the fault of the governmental form. Our purpose here is not to address the problems that arise from the lack of quality in the men in positions of leadership. Our desire is first to see the pattern itself, and realize that altering the pattern is not the solution to resolving the problems that exists in the hearts of men.

It would be a mistake to think that *the* pattern for overseeing churches on the local church level is *always* expressed in the form of strong leader type pastor. It would be equally wrong to look at the churches in the earliest stages like Acts chapter fourteen and make this the final answer for governing churches, *especially if we do this without the guidance of apostles or bishops*. It was not the final answer then because they were still experiencing development and change in the episcopate. On the local church level, they were experiencing continual development within the body of elders. In some churches, brethren in five-fold ministry were joined to the churches and became a part of the eldership. And in some churches some of those initially ordained elders began to emerge as those called to the diaconate. On higher levels of administration, bishops were added *in some cases*. Also, the involvement of apostles in overseeing roles increased or diminished, depending on the need.

Therefore, in all of this let us realize the importance of a functioning body of elders in the local church. At the same time, let us recognize an underlying principle for shepherding in both the Old and the New Testament—the principle of "a man". And let us make allowance in the church life today for the various forms of this principle to be expressed—to be expressed according to the need.

Having made a case for the role of a lead-man overseer, I want to conclude this chapter by looking at the ministry of James, the Lord's brother, and make a couple of observations. In Acts chapter fifteen we have the council where Paul and Barnabas met with the apostles and elders at Jerusalem. Many things were voiced in that meeting, but it was settled when James spoke. The impression is clearly that his input brought finality to the issue being considered. Some view the "finality" simply as an indication of the anointing upon James *for that occasion*. What they see in this is not a man in a "position" of leadership, but a man in authority *when he is anointed*. However, there are a number of references to indicate that over a period of years James was recognized in the role of lead-man in the midst of those elders (Acts 12:17; 21:18; Galatians 2:12). There is no hint that this recognition is so delicate as to hinge upon a meeting by meeting experience. It is not defined in terms of how anointed James is on each occasion the elders come together, but more in terms of a "position" he occupied in that body of leaders.

We have sought to define episcopate in a way so as to avoid the image of "offices" within a hierarchy. Nevertheless, it is not possible to remove altogether the fact that this lead-man's role is realized in a "position" or "spot" within the relationships of that overseeing body, or within that congregation. Obviously if the man in that "position" is not functioning with some degree of consistent anointing, something is not right. It is possible he is not in the right "position". That would need to be assessed.

But on the other hand, to envision this role as him being the most anointed man within the group, or the one through whom God always brings His word to the elders—to view it that way would be too idealistic and hoping for too much. Thus, my first observation is that the lead-man's role is realized in a "position" and not merely as the one who is most anointed on each occasion the overseers come together.

The second observation relates to James's ministry in the sense of Ephesians 4:11. He was an apostle. Sometimes those who have difficulty acknowledging the lead-man are balking at the idea that anyone other than a pastor in the Ephesians 4:11 category could ever be in this role. In other words, "pastor" in Ephesians 4:11 means these are the ones to feed the local flock. In taking that position they are not making a definite distinction between the dynamic of the measure of gifting and the measure of the rule. They cannot visualize a "pastor" as one given trans-locally to the Body of Christ. To them, he is only pastor in the setting of sheep-shepherd relationships. And to have one of the other five-fold ministry involved in local churches in a lead role—to them it does not make sense. I trust that the problems of this limited view of "pastor" are obvious. Too many things about the operation of the Lord's church just will not fit if we view "pastor" that way.

I am sure that we can say that those who are Ephesians 4:11 pastors have within their gifting the things that would best qualify *them* to be the feeders in local churches. Nevertheless, we cannot say that those other four ministries cannot be in the lead-man role, or even that it is not God's will for them to do that. It would be convenient if all churches came into existence by well-formed strategy. If we were going to send a church planting team to the next town, we could make it a part of the strategy to see a certain man who is Ephesians 4:11 pastor come into the position of the lead-man for that new congregation. But the reality of it is that many churches come into being by a different process. The church at Antioch came into being as the result of persecuted believers fleeing to that area and being faithful to share their faith. Likewise, the church at Samaria was birthed through the preaching of an evangelist who came there to avoid persecution. Church history abounds with these examples.

In the case of Philip in Samaria, he yielded his role in that new work when the two apostles from Jerusalem arrived. Suppose that those two brothers did not come. There have certainly been many cases that would correspond to that. Would it be inappropriate for Philip as an evangelist to remain in Samaria and proceed to shepherd those sheep? Or after he has been shepherding them for a number of years, is it necessarily the Lord's plan for him to yield that role to a bonafide pastor? Certainly not! Some people seem to have that mentality, though. When evangelists, prophets or any of the ministry have faithfully given themselves to feeding sheep and the Lord has worked with them in that arrangement, how can anyone say it is wrong? Of course if, the lead-man is only an evangelist in his diaconate and he does not realize the importance of the supply of those other Ephesians 4:11 ministries also, eventually the lack will manifest itself in the response of the sheep. But the same could be said of the teacher or the prophet who pastors. The Lord did not intend that the lead-man in a local church have all the gifts, or be the only one through whom the sheep are fed. Elders also should feed the sheep. Thus my second observation is that the lead-man is not necessarily an Ephesians 4:11 pastor, but could possibly be any one of those five. Which one it will be is to a great extent determined by a historical process presided over and confirmed by the Ascended Christ.

CHAPTER **8**

THE COUNSEL OF PEACE

"Behold a man whose name is Branch...He will build the temple of the Lord...will bear the honor and sit and rule on His throne. Thus, He will be a priest on His throne, and the counsel of peace will be between the two offices" (Zechariah 6:12-13).

In this Messianic promise the prophet is looking forward to the time when civil government and religious government of Israel will no longer be so completely separated. With the Advent of the Son, God the Father will have found a condition where the headship of both of these offices can be safely vested in one Person. To describe the quality of that joining he makes the interesting statement that there will be peace between the two offices. I want to take that statement out of the context of the "offices" Zechariah is talking about and apply the thought to the two things we have discussed—the diaconate and the episcopate.

It is apparent that some of the problems in church government arise out of a lack of understanding of the distinctiveness of those two leadership roles and of the dynamics that correspond to each: the measure of the gift and the measure of the rule. In that regard I suppose one of the greatest problems is men being in one role and presuming upon the other. Some men are overseers, but not in the Ephesians 4:11 category. Others are in that category, but not in oversight. It often happens that these leaders attempt to expand their leadership role from the one into the other without really being called or without fulfilling the conditions. There are a number of ways I could illustrate this, but will refrain for now and concentrate on one aspect of the possible conflicts of these two "offices".

Some men are ordained of God to be in both diaconate and episcopate. Yet, however sincere and nobly they give themselves to both, there will inevitably be tensions between the two. I want to illustrate this in the life of Paul using the occasion of his writing the Corinthians as their apostolic overseer while aspiring to do more to fulfill his trans-local calling in ministry.

"For we are not overextending ourselves, as if we did not reach to you, for we were the first to come even as far as you in the gospel of Christ; not boasting beyond our measure, that is, in other men's labors, but with the hope that as your faith grows, we shall be, within our sphere, enlarged even more by you, so as to preach the gospel even to the regions beyond you..." (II Corinthians 10:14-16).

Earlier in the same letter Paul describes the struggle he felt when he arrived at Troas and had an open door for ministry, but was hindered because of his involvement with the Corinthians (II Corinthians 2:12-13). Paul was a real example of a team player and always preferred to do things with coworkers. But he could do it alone, and he did so once before (e.g. at Mar's Hill in Athens). Not having Titus to help was not the issue, but Titus' present mission was. He had been sent to Corinth to appeal to them to repent and Paul was anxiously awaiting Titus' return to know how they had responded (II Corinthians 7:5-7). In that case Paul was already at Troas and the limitation he felt was an emotional one only. Now Paul is considering the prospect of going to regions beyond and will feel logistical limitations unless something happens and he is released from the sense of responsibility he feels toward them. So, first of all, let us consider the two factors by which Paul determined the extent of his involvement and the extent of his release.

The first principle concerns the growth of their faith. How sad it is to see situations where overseers cultivate in their followers an unwholesome dependence upon their leadership. A true overseer of the Lord's heritage should be desirous for the sheep to grow into maturity and not be so dependent on him. He does not wish to rule over their faith, but rather that they have the "joy" of doing things for themselves (II Corinthians 1:24). He looks for them to take more responsibility in evangelizing. He expects them to sacrifice their own goods to see the work supported. Even in the governing of the church, they are to feel a responsibility. Obviously, the more they take responsibility in these things, the more the overseer is freed to devote his energies in other directions.

The second principle is "that we shall be enlarged by you." More literally this should read, "that we shall be magnified in (or among) you." This is the same word used in Acts 5:13 where it says of the apostles that the people magnified them. Why should Paul be desiring something like that from this church? Is he being vain, or wanting glory from man? Hardly! And yet, not only regarding this church, but regarding others also, he was quite concerned about what they were thinking about him. (e.g. I Corinthians 1:11; II Corinthians 1:14; 5:11; 7:2-7; 10:10; 11:16; 12:11; Galatians 4:12-16; I Thessalonians 3:5-6; II Timothy 1:8). What is the explanation for this?

Overseers have close relationships with the ones who follow them. It is *primarily* by their example that overseers influence the sheep. The enemy's strategy is, "smite the shepherd and the sheep will scatter." In other words, slander the pastor and the sheep will stumble. Belittle the overseer's ministry and those under his care will become discouraged. It is interesting to note that all of the scriptures just listed involved disciples or churches *under Paul's overseership only*. In the case of groups which were not under Paul's care (but which may have been slandering him), I doubt seriously that he would show any concern for what they were thinking of him. Paul's heart in these matters is revealed in his closing words of this epistle.

"Now I pray to God that ye do no evil; not that we should appear approved, but that ye should do that which is honest, though we be as reprobates. For we can do nothing against the truth, but for the truth" (II Corinthians 13:7-8).

The highest concern of the Lord's servant is for the sheep to walk in truth. There is a sense in which the truth stands entirely on its own apart from the man. Now if the sheep are discerning enough to always recognize truth and embrace it *completely distinct from the messengers of it*, this would be most wonderful! That was Paul's hope. Even if they considered him a reprobate, he was satisfied as long as it did not affect their attitude toward the truth. Unfortunately, it is not that simple. Usually if the sheep look disparagingly upon the messenger, neither can they appreciate his message. They find it even harder to submit to the man's bishopric. The purpose of the enemy in these "smitings" is apparent. He is seeking to cut off the leaders from the people. The leader's motive in making such a defense to the people is *only* to prevent that operation, nothing more. Now, let us put all of this together in light of those two principles.

On the one hand Paul was desirous that their faith increase. He wanted them to mature to the extent that it required less oversight from him. On the other hand, he did not want this process to be "short-circuited." If they did not continue to hold him (and his ministry) in the proper esteem, that is what would happen. In an unwholesome way, in a way unnatural to the normal process of maturing as a local body, they would become independent. Whether these Corinthians realized it or not, they still needed Paul's oversight on this higher level of administration. Therefore, the balance of these factors is what guided this apostle in knowing whether or not he was to continue to focus his energies in a place, or to stretch forth to regions beyond. If their faith had increased to a certain level, and if they continued to hold him in esteem, then he was free to look to new territories. Thankfully, that is what happened. After arriving at Corinth and spending some time with them, he writes to Rome stating that he has "no more place" in those parts and is looking for new territory (Romans 15:23-24).

In the case of Paul's critics at Corinth, their criticism was unfounded. Paul had faithfully fulfilled what is required for an overseer to have the rule which the Lord distributed to him. Unfortunately, some of the Lord's servants today have not been so blameless in this charge. They, perhaps innocently, have sought to stretch forth into new areas of ministry without fulfilling what is required of them in the former works. Principles are violated and feelings become strained between the people and the leaders. We have already described the three functions that characterize the way Christ distributes the rule. And we said that the expression of that shepherding is not only developed initially by those three functions, but maintained by them. We want to look now more specifically at things that pertain to this maintenance.

One principle concerns replacing of leadership. If a sphere of oversight is to be expanded, there must be men to step into places of responsibility formerly borne by the leader who is now stretching forth. (Wise is the leader who has a constant eye open for future overseers from within the flock! For his "crown" is not forever. Proverbs 27:23-24). Two things need to be considered. One is to pick the most qualified man as far as ministerial ability is concerned; the other concerns the relationship of this new overseer to the former one. If in stretching forth to new areas it is right before the Lord for this first leader to still retain some measure of oversight over the former work, then I say that the second consideration is the more important one. If a man is selected for the work on the basis of ministerial ability, but he himself does not come under the oversight of the former leader, then the right to retain the rule there is being forfeited. You see, even though this man has already developed that special relationship with those sheep, it has not been developed with the new leader. Therefore, Christian ethics demand that the new overseer be respected as an individual servant before his own Master, to be guided and directed by Him. Let us illustrate this.

Paul, Silas, and Timothy come as a team to Macedonia. At Thessalonica heavy persecution sets in and Paul is forced to flee to Athens. Soon thereafter he sends commandment for the brethren to join him there. Paul was forced to separate from the Thessalonians prematurely. He urgently desired to get back to this new church. In lieu of his going, one of these brethren is sent. As far as *ability* is concerned, Silas would have been the logical choice. He formerly was recognized for his prophetic office; now he is an apostle. However, Paul sends Timothy. I marvel at this, for about twelve years after this Timothy was considered to be a young man for the ministry he was doing (I Timothy 4:12). How very young he must have been when he started! He was not only young in age, but also in experience. Not even one year has transpired from the time that he joined this team till the time he is on his way alone back to Thessalonica! Moreover, one of the things he is sent to do in this infant church is to "establish" them (1 Thessalonians 3:2)! This choice of Timothy might seem strange to us if we do not understand Paul's strategy.

Timothy, Titus, and such brethren had a unique relationship with Paul. He aggressively took leadership in their lives. These brethren freely chose to have this relationship with him. In a sense, because of the relationship, Paul is "using" them. He did not hesitate to employ them to serve him and to do things to further the work *the Lord had given him to do.* In my opinion, Paul was not very concerned with training these brethren so that they could have *their ministry.* ("...for he is profitable *to me* for the ministry." (II Timothy 4:11). Yet on the other hand, if these brethren faithfully fulfilled the opportunities that opened to them through their relationship with Paul, in a natural way "their" ministry would develop; they would receive "their own" (Luke 16:12). Thus, because of the unique relationship of these young brothers with him, Paul sent them to various churches as delegates representing his ministry; he sent them to contend for his way (I Corinthians 4:17). He was able to "use" them as an extension of his episcopate.

Silas did not have that kind of relationship with Paul. He was a peer brother working alongside Paul fulfilling the two-by-two principle practiced in the early church. He acknowledged Paul as the head of the team and they worked together to get a job done. Nevertheless, he was a minister in his own right and worthy of acceptance in that kind of "equality." It simply meant that Paul could not relate to him in the same way that he did to those younger brethren. Hence, I am impressed with the fact that more than once Paul sent these very young brethren to the churches to do jobs above their own capabilities. He did it at the risk of them not being received (and on some occasions they were not)! Also, he did it when more qualified ministers apparently were available. He did it, however, for good reason.

A second principle relates to the functions of meaningful involvement and also watching. That is, the overseer must truly be knowledgeable of the condition of those under his care and the sheep must be reassured of this. When Paul gathered the elders at Ephesus to exhort them about their charge, he told them that lawlessness would come into the flock by wolves from without and ambitious men from within. Possibly he said this on the basis of problems that come to any church, but more likely he was personally cognizant of who those perverse men were. And when he heard of the divisions at Corinth, he was not surprised ("...in part, I believe it." (I Corinthians 11:18). I want to say right here that rebellion in a flock does not necessarily reflect on the quality of the overseer's work, *but ignorance of the conditions leading up to it does*. God himself permitted a rebellion in heaven, but He surely knew it was coming. For overseeing to be effective, it is so important that overseers know the true condition of their flocks. They should diligently seek to know what is happening by the means which are available to them.

One of the means available to these leaders is purely spiritual revelation. The Lord can reveal things to an overseer *even when he is physically separated from the area* and involved elsewhere. The Lord revealed to Moses on the summit of the mount what the Israelites were doing in his absence. Paul had access to that kind of spiritual knowing (Colossians 2:1-5). However, it can create a "temptation" to these overseers to rely too much upon this means of "knowing" and thereby justify their being absent too long from their area of oversight. A healthy work properly developed should be able to bear the absence of the shepherd some, but how much? However "spiritual" he is and capable of watching in times of absence, that knowing cannot release him from the need of his being involved with those sheep. Those sheep within that rule must be able to feel from their hearts that their overseer is sufficiently involved to really know what is going on. If they do not feel that he is well informed of the situation, they will lose confidence in his decisions and that rule will begin to break down. He may, indeed, know the situation better then they realize, but that is not enough. As the overseer reaches forth into new areas, he must continue to do things in the former flock in such a way that the sheep are confident that he really knows their state.

A third principle is also related to the overseer being involved in a meaningful way. That is, his availability in their hour of need. When a disciple or church is in a crisis, if the overseer is to still be involved with them according to the measure of the rule, he must be available for help. There is a natural process for new churches to learn to get answers for their problems from the Lord. Yet, often this process is forced to "maturity" sooner than it should be. When these believers are forced to struggle on their own to get the answers for their problems, *they have been forced to become independent* of the rule they formerly were helped by!

There is a restful way for churches to grow to a place of less dependence upon the overseer. How unfortunate when the neglect or unrealistic planning of the overseer hinders this process from coming about in a seemly fashion. But even when he has faithfully fulfilled what is required of him for maintaining the rule, there will be times when lawlessness will seek to turn the sheep against their shepherd. Rebellion was brewing at Corinth. Paul resorted to letters and messengers first to try to handle the problems. When those measures failed, he personally was ready to follow through with a visit to deal with the problems (II Corinthians 13:1-2). However, had he not been to do so, I do not think that he could talk about a rule *which still reached to them*.

This brings us to an important question in our study: Does the fact that a leader was the first one in a work or in discipling a person *establish* a rule over them?

> **For we are not overextending ourselves, as if we did not reach to you, for we were the *first* to come even as far as you in the gospel of Christ...For in Christ Jesus I have begotten you through the gospel" (II Corinthians 10:14; I Corinthians 4:15)**.

Certainly, being "first" has *some* significance in God's kingdom as the potential beginning of a new rule. However, in the passing of time, making claim to that *only* and not fulfilling other things cannot establish a rule toward a people. If Paul's case rested *only* on the fact that he was the one who led the Corinthians into the kingdom, it is doubtful that he could have regained control there. But he had been faithful in all of these points. That blamelessness gave a solid platform for the Holy Spirit to work there and break the power of the rebellion.

In conclusion, let us realize that there are tensions in the interaction of the diaconate and the episcopate. A lot of this can be relieved just by gaining a clear comprehension of the distinctiveness of each role. As I said in the beginning of this chapter, being in one role and presuming upon the other is a problem. We will illustrate this further in the next two chapters. But not only that, many are in both roles and, like Paul, experience a tension between the two. Both of these roles are so important for Christ to govern His Church. May God grant us wisdom and understanding that we may experience peace in the interaction of the two!

CHAPTER 9

LOCAL AND EXTRA-LOCAL AUTHORITY

In this chapter and the next we want to consider the relationship of the sphere of government of local churches and the sphere of government of ministry operating trans-locally. More specifically we want to see how these two spheres mutually interact without "violating" each other. Here in the discussion of the five-fold ministry, we are not concerning ourselves with apostles in oversight relationships or men functioning in the role of bishops. Those overseers have their governmental roles towards those particular churches defined by the measure of the rule. What we want to look at now is the case of minsters who do not have that. How do they relate to the churches and how do the churches relate to them? To do this we want to study the situation of those five minsters gathering together at Antioch (Acts 13:1-3).

First of all, it is important to see that this gathering of men was not just another meeting under the umbrella of the eldership at Antioch. Any church that has been around for a while and has grown is going to have committees and meetings. All of these in one way or another will be under the government of the church eldership and accountable to them. But this gathering was more than a committee meeting. It was not functioning under the umbrella of the eldership, nor was it the eldership meeting. Some might take issue with that since they have used this to make a case that all elders are in the five-fold ministry (This will be discussed in some detail in chapter thirteen) However, in saying that this was not and eldership meeting, I am not saying that those men were not in the eldership.

It is reasonable for any of the five-fold ministry who are going to be "planted" for a season in a local church to become a part of that eldership. It is reasonable, but not automatic. The measure of the gift which Christ has distributed to them—a measure which places them in a governmental role—does not automatically carry with it the governmental role of the episcopate. If it is God's will for them to be one of the elders, they must give themselves to the same functions of overseeing as those other brethren. They cannot presume upon the authority of their ministry office that they are a part of that episcopate while they are there; it must be developed.

If those five brethren *were* a part of the eldership, they had dual roles. Here in this gathering we see them in their role simply as those whom Christ has given trans-locally. The very "business" of their meeting was trans-local in nature. They were not coming together seeking strategy for taking the city. Technically speaking, the Antioch Church should feel that responsibility. The responsibility these men felt is what all of the five-fold ministry should feel. Evangelism is the "business" of the whole church, but God requires the ministry to lead the way (I Corinthians 9:16-17); especially to take the gospel to regions beyond.

The procedures of their meetings were distinct from the governing process of the Antioch Church. I do not know how many times these brethren had come together like this before this final session. In any case, there is no intimation that their decisions were going to be submitted to the eldership for approval. Indeed, it seems that this gathering constituted an autonomy of its own. Whatever they decided under God had a finality about it. Moreover, they were prepared to bear the responsibility for the workability of it. Their plans did not require the manpower or finances of that local church.

When the decision was finalized, the two brethren were set apart for "the work." That phrase means more than merely the fact that they were going out to work. A precise concept of apostolic ministry is surely envisioned in these words (Acts 13:2; 14:26; 15:38). This raises important questions: Did the eldership at Antioch feel a responsibility to oversee the ministry of those two apostles? Did they feel that they were in some way "over" the churches planted by those apostles? I think not! I have already mentioned in chapter two that when the Antioch Church commended those men to God's grace, they were acknowledging their qualifications and preparedness to embark on that mission. But I think this act of commending is a declaration of something else also. The local elders were acknowledging that the work of the two apostles was a trans-local ministry and out of their jurisdiction. But I see no reason to limit this to apostolic work only. Any of the five-fold ministry that have experience and maturity that qualifies them to operate trans-locally and live by the gospel should be respected in that role. It is unseemly for a local church to feel that they have to be "over" that ministry when it is operating trans-locally.

It says that *they* fasted and prayed, and *they* sent them away. Who are the "they"? After the Holy Spirit revealed His will to those five men, or after they had a time of fasting and prayer to confirm the message, did they adjourn and later reassemble with the whole church? In other words, does it mean that the local church was sending out those two brothers? When they completed *the work*, they returned "to Antioch, from which they had been commended to the grace of God..." "Antioch" might imply the church in that city, but it is more likely in the narrative of those chapters to be one more reference to the cities listed in their places of travel. In other words, "Antioch" is where it happened, but does not tell us who did the commending. It is in the next verse that Luke tells us of their gathering together with the church (Acts 14:26-27). Thus, should we not expect the "they" to be referring to this ministerial group in each of those statements? That is to say, the sending agent was that ministerial group. This is the more reasonable interpretation to me.

Luke is careful to mention details. In chapter fifteen we have the occasion of the Jerusalem council. We are specifically told that the church received (and we might add "hosted") those men, along with the apostles and elders. But when it comes to assembling to deal with the business at hand, the church is not mentioned (Acts 15:4-6). I do not wish to split hairs, or seem to totally divorce the activity of ministerial groups from local churches. It is good stewardship when ministerial groups can share the facilities with local churches. It is loving and gracious for the churches to host these groups, to say nothing of fulfilling the need of God's servants for fellowship. Paul was certainly diligent to solicit this from the church at Rome (Romans 15:22-25). It would be a great loss to the kingdom of God for churches to be left out, or not feel a part of *the work.*

Moreover, in some of the descriptions in the Acts concerning ministries travelling out, it would be hard from the narrative to make a case that they were not being sent out by the churches. But this picture in chapter thirteen appears to be unique. A number of principles that are to guide the order of the church can be found here. The one I wish to establish now is that *there is an autonomy in ministerial groupings that cannot be ruled over by the eldership of local churches.* Having said that, I must mention that there are groups that do not acknowledge this and yet appear to really be effective in their work for the kingdom of God.

The groups which are ruled over by local elderships usually have a sound vision for team ministry. If possible, they try to put together teams that include all five ministries. However, they envision this all to be under the "umbrella" of a local church. Often that will mean that the members of the team will have a dual role. They will be part of the staff of that church and most likely will be salaried by the church; in the outworkings of this, they are sent out by that church. The more noble ones with this vision see it as their mission to send out teams to outlying areas to help smaller groups who cannot afford to have a staff with all five ministries, which is often very helpful to these smaller groups. These sending churches will bear the expenses of these ventures and will not try to bring those other churches "under" them. There is much to be said to the credit of the way they are doing things. But the bottom line of their concept is that the five-fold ministry is under the eldership of local churches. There are probably good reasons why these groups maintain this posture.

Possibly these churches have reacted to the deadness and the cumbersomeness of the hierarchy of older denominations. They feel that independent, local churches are the focal point of what God is doing. Yet, having aspired to be independent, they probably have also seen abuses in expressions of extra-local authority. They are turned off by some who lay claim to apostleship, but have demonstrated it poorly. And as for bishops, they relegate that to the past as an innovation of men to replace the first apostles. To be sure, when extra-local overseers are abusive, or misguided, there is safety in pulling back and keeping everything under the umbrella of the local church. But we cannot concern ourselves here with abuses or excesses. We must find the pattern for the way Christ seeks to govern His Church.

At the heart of the issue of the autonomy of the ministry is financial support. Paul did not hesitate to speak of the reasonableness of his being helped by those who benefitted from his ministry. He made a strong case concerning our right to live by the gospel. Yet at the same time, he spoke much of his freedom as a minister of Christ. How dearly he cherished it! He preferred rather to deny himself of the right to live by the gospel and work with his own hands than to forego that freedom (I Corinthians 9:1-18). It would appear that when men are salaried by one local church it creates a temptation to them to "come under" the church in a way which forfeits that "freedom". And it creates a temptation to the church to watch over their investment. Consequently, the terms by which ministers receive financial help must be discerned and men must be willing to deny themselves, if necessary, in order to not forfeit that freedom.

Having made the point concerning the "freedom" of the five-fold ministry, I do not wish to remove the necessity of their being accountable. Accountability is important! There is a difference between the eldership overseeing the *life* of these men and overseeing the *ministry* of these men. In churches where ministries are based, it is reasonable for the elders to feel a concern for the welfare of those men and their families. To have men watching their life style, and observing their testimony is a wholesome arrangement. Moreover, I am not seeking to make a case that encourages ministers to work trans-locally as individuals. The early church was zealous for team ministry. It is the Holy Spirit's agenda today to get ministers joined in the right relationships. When this happens as it did with those five at Antioch, let us see it as an autonomous entity designed to express one aspect of the kingdom of God, an entity that is not to be brought "under" the governing of local churches.

CHAPTER 10

MORE ABOUT ELDERS

In the previous chapter we discussed the prospect of the five-fold ministry being part of the eldership of a local church. We concluded that this could not be presumed because of the authority of their diaconate, but something that must be developed. How about a higher level of administration? Remember, we are not talking about ministers who are bishops, or apostolic overseers. We are looking at the general way that the five-fold ministry moves about trans-locally and trying to understand how they relate to churches. Is there a general sense in which they are overseers of the Body of Christ? Can we think of them as elders at large? There are groups that espouse the view that those in these ministry capacities *are* elders to the Body.

There are four instances cited which might seem to support that position. However, in each instance other reasons can be given for referring to those men as elders; none of these four are really conclusive. Two cases are Peter and John who refer to themselves as elders (I Peter 5:1; II John 1;3). There are references in early church writings which speak of the original twelve as elders of the church. If this John was John the Beloved, that would account for a special sense that these two thought of themselves as being elders. Moreover, at the time he wrote the epistles, John would have the unique honor of being the only survivor of the twelve. Hence, *the elder*. And even if that is not the case, there is no reason to think that this John did not have an overseeing relationship developed with that church (e.g. their bishop or apostle). The content of the letters certainly suggests that kind of familiarity. Besides the two cases of Peter and John, there is the instance of Paul writing to Philemon and referring to himself as "aged" (Philemon 8-10). If, as some think, that word is referring to an office (e.g. "elder") and not merely to his age, Paul did not regard it as carrying much authority when soliciting Philemon's obedience. He merely mentions this "agedness" and appeals to other things to enjoin Philemon. In reality, with Epaphras as his liaison, Paul still retained a measure of apostolic oversight with the churches in that area. And then finally there is one more case cited which to me is the most interesting.

In the first chapter of Acts we see the Eleven assembled and waiting upon God for direction to find a replacement for Judas. Peter is explicit that they are looking for one, and only one replacement (v. 20, 24). How are we to understand that? Is there a limit to the number of those original apostles? The New Jerusalem has as part of its foundation the twelve apostles of the Lamb (Revelation 21:14). Some have tried to discredit the method in which Matthias was chosen and thereby suggest that the Holy Spirit did not confirm it. The Holy Writ acknowledges him as one of the Twelve (Acts 6:2). Even if we were to eliminate Matthias, we still would have more than twelve. James, the Lord's brother, was in their ranks (I Corinthians 15:7; Galatians 1:19). And Paul claimed that he was not lesser in rank with that group (I Corinthians 15:9; II Corinthians 11:5; 12:11). Moreover, recall what we said in chapter two about the five-fold ministry. The giving of the office *is not determined or defined by an immediate need*. It is true that this original apostleship was given for a season during the early part of Church history, but there is no reason to assert that during that season there could only be a certain number of these apostles *as far as diaconate is concerned*. We can only resolve this by recognizing that the Judas apostasy created a vacancy in another way.

Peter said, "His office (lit. position as overseer) let another take" (v. 20). I have already said that the Twelve had the recognition of being *The Elders* in the tradition of the early church. If we will recall some of the things the Lord said to them, and words of the prophets, we will understand their vision (Matthew 19:28; Luke 22:29-30; Isaiah 24:23). These specially chosen apostles sitting upon twelve thrones were a unique kind of eldership! Concerning diaconate, there was no particular number for this original group, but concerning episcopate—only twelve. If this be true, how can we appeal to this very unique situation for a pattern and say that today all of the five-fold ministry likewise are *the elders* to the Body of Christ?

It would be conflicting and confusing to talk of some ministers who have developed relationships with particular churches as extra-local overseers and then to allow that any other five-fold ministry is also an "overseer" to those churches. That would be the significance of that concept because elders, by the very meaning of the office, are overseers in shepherding roles. I think that it is significant that Old Testament prophets were never referred to as one of the groups of Israel's shepherds. Priests were referred to that way. Jeremiah who was a priest later laments that it was not his choice to leave pastoring to become a part of the prophetic office (Jeremiah 17:16). There is definitely an aspect of government invested in the measure of the gift which Christ has distributed to the five-fold ministry, but "elder" or "overseer" just does not describe it. We should not think of them in their trans-local ministry as being "over" the Church like that.

In the initial stages the Lord uses ministry to plant churches. But once eldership is appointed those churches have attained an autonomy. Having received that responsibility it is incumbent upon those elders to examine the credentials of those claiming to be ministers of Christ. Paul warned the elders at Ephesus to be watchful. Later on we see them approved by John for having been diligent to do that (Acts 20:28-30; Revelation 2:2). The things discussed in the previous chapter concerning the autonomy of trans-local ministry must be understood in the light of what we are considering now. The eldership of local churches do not, on the one hand, have the right to oversee the trans-local ministry of the diaconate. But on the other hand, they must feel the responsibility to be watchful when ministers come to the church. They are the overseers. And having checked the credentials and found them to be true servants of Christ, there is responsibility upon them as to how they are going to receive these servants. A serious matter for the churches (Matthew 10:40-41)! Even so, receiving ministry cannot be imposed upon them. Those whom Christ has given trans-locally to the Body must respect the autonomy of local churches. Finally, let us look at one more aspect of eldership to the Body at large.

I have tried to show that ministers coming to a church for a season are not elders there just by virtue of their Ephesians 4:11 office. And I trust I have established that they are not elders to the Body at large. Yet there is much talk today about leaders being elders in a city, meaning not only the congregations in that city for which they are directly responsible, but a kind of oversight of the whole city. There is also talk about national leaders—ministers who gain credibility across the nation and are respected by large segments of the church for their wisdom. Sometimes these men are referred to as "fathers." It would seem that Paul reserved the usage of that word just for men who had working relationships developed with particular churches (I Corinthians 4:14-21). Probably "elders" would be a better way to identify these national leaders. But what about this? God knows there is a cry in the Church today for these senior brethren to come forth, but can we substantiate from Scripture such an "office"?

Unless Peter and Paul when referring to themselves had this kind of eldership in mind in those instances we cited above, I know of nothing else to point to in the New Testament for such a precedent. Even so, I think referring to national brethren as elders is harmonious with the ways of the Lord if we define it correctly. Recall what was said in chapter four about the difference between general elders and official (or governing) elders. General elders are not appointed. They earn their own credibility with the people. And of necessity, they earn it because they have a history of faithfulness, integrity and true spiritual authority. Furthermore, because they are not part of the official eldership, there must be a limitation upon the extent they guide the congregation. But within those limitations they can have a powerful influence. If we think of these national leaders as "elders" in the same sense as these general elders have their role in a local congregation, I see no problem, but rather a great asset for the Church. This means that we are not ascribing to these men an official authority like overseers through whom Christ distributes a measure of rule. But on the other hand, neither does our defining it this way limit the Lord's sovereign prerogative to stand with these men and confirm the things they say.

Also, I do not believe we should encourage men to try to bring forth these leaders by forming their own "networks" or organizations and promoting them. It is seemly for them to earn that status and come into that recognition by the approval of the Lord. Let the Lord raise up these senior brethren regionally and nationally the same way that He raises general elders locally.

In conclusion, we are allowing for the prospect of not all, but some of the five-fold ministry, to be elders to the Body at large. And the reason they are in that position is not merely because they are in the ministry, but because they have been faithfully in it for many years and gained respect for their maturity. And for the rest of the ministry of Christ, they are those who are given trans-locally and who do have an aspect of government towards the whole church. We do not define that as their being "over" the church like overseers, but see it functioning in other ways.

So, to more clearly define these positions, we must look at the nature of the authority of the diaconate and the authority of the episcopate. But before doing that, let us take one more chapter and consider an expression of government that is not local church administration, nor does it fit into extra-local administration as we have discussed it thus far.

CHAPTER 11

THE PRESBYTERY

In this chapter I want to explore another expression of church government that was practiced in the early church. We find this mentioned in a statement Paul makes to Timothy reminding him of part of the process that facilitated his being launched into a trans-local ministry.

"Do not neglect the spiritual gift within you, which was bestowed upon you through the laying on of hands by the presbytery" (I Timothy 4:14).

Let us begin with a word study.

Thus far in our study on elders we have been working with one word "presbuteros," and usually in the plural form. We have explained it as the title for a body of men set into local churches as the overseers. Then in the previous chapter we considered the possible ways that men on extra-local levels of administration might by regarded as elders. In that prospect also it is defined by the use of this one word translated as elders. However, in the verse quoted above Paul employs a different Greek word, "presbuterion". This is a neuter form of "presbuteros" but *definitely a different word*. I emphasize that because often this slips the attention of some and they treat it as an alternate way of referring to the plural form of "elder." If that is all that is intended, then we might picture Timothy's send-off as being a gathering of elders in one local church (with possibly Paul and some other ministers in attendance). I believe that Paul intentionally chose this different word in order to convey a particular concept about church government.

This word translated "presbytery" only occurs two other times in the New Testament. With so little scripture to work with, we cannot be dogmatic. On the other hand, seeing how much importance Paul attaches to it, neither can we afford to ignore it. The other two references are Luke 22:66 and Acts 22:5, where in both cases it refers to a particular aspect of the government of the Jewish nation. The NAS renders it "council of elders" and for a marginal note has "board of elders" for this presbytery Timothy was blessed by. In the case of the Jewish nation, it is not clear to me if this is another way of referring to the Sanhedrin, who were the contemporary expression of that official body of elders instituted with Moses—the Seventy, or, if it is a combination of the Sanhedrin and other leaders. Regardless, it was an official body of men with governing power. It was not just a group of general elders from the various tribes and cities gathering together for some particular occasion.

Of the churches I am acquainted with, (outside of the historical denominations) to my knowledge there are two ways in which "presbytery" is employed to identify some governmental function or practice. To develop this study, I want to discuss those two practices and compare them with what we might glean from these few verses of scripture.

The first practice concerns gatherings that are devoted to getting a prophetic word for the people. This is not referring to the general kind of prophesying of the believers to one another— prophecies which are encouraging and exhortational but not so specific as to give direction to people's lives. Rather, this is a more serious endeavor for the purpose of getting specific words from God—prophecies which are directional or governmental in nature. To accomplish this, effort is made to have (usually from outside the episcopate) one or two men recognized for their prophetic gifting. In this controlled arrangement under the umbrella of local church eldership the Lord has been pleased in recent years to bless His church. How does this compare with Timothy's case?

If we add to this I Timothy 1:18 and if this is referring to the presbytery, then two things were happening: prophesying and laying on of hands. It is possible that the prophesying was from one or two prophets attending that gathering, and that the laying on of hands was a time when the presbyters confirmed the prophesies with their prayers and blessing. That would imply that the "prophets" were not necessarily the presbyters and the presbyters were not necessarily the ones prophesying. However, most of the teachings I am familiar with assume that it was the presbyters doing the prophesying while they laid hands on Timothy. The question is, who were they? Were they men (from outside) called in because of the prophetic gifting and in that setting regarded as presbyters? I find it difficult to establish that by any other practices of the early church.

Since the word for presbyter is from the root word for elder, we expect it in some way to correlate with the concept of elder and all that pertains to that role. In the previous chapter we discussed the difficulty of regarding men in the diaconate as being elders to parts of the body where shepherding relationships are not developed. Usually the prophets today who are called in are "outsiders" to the sphere of oversight of the sheep that will be ministered to in the presbytery meeting. Moreover, we regard that as advantageous. It is effective for believers to receive prophecy from ministers who know little or nothing about them. To receive words from those who shepherd us—well, we are tempted to not regard that with the same gravity since we can reason that they are not speaking from special revelation of the Spirit, but out of their personal knowledge of us.

In Timothy's case, when it was time for him to be sent with Paul, we have only a brief explanation of the steps. (Acts 16:1-3) There were three churches that were closely situated geographically: Derbe, Lystra, and Iconium. The brethren of two of these churches recommended Timothy to Paul. That means that on a small scale at least Timothy was moving about in those churches and known by those elders. Assuming that Paul was reminding Timothy of that presbytery because he personally was there, other than this Acts sixteen incident I see no other occasion when it could have happened. Moreover, if the presbytery was a gathering of the leaders in only one of those churches, I see no reason for Paul to choose another word and not use the usual word for elders. In other words, it would be like any service today when the elders come together (possibly with any five-fold ministry travelling through at that time) and lay hands on someone. I suspect that this presbytery was a gathering of elders from at least the two churches recommending Timothy, and probably all three.

There is the possibility that Paul was not in the presbytery he was reminding Timothy of. That is, there had been a presbytery prior to this time Timothy joined Paul and he later learned from Timothy or some of those elders about the prophecies. And now at this crucial time in Timothy's life, Paul is reminding him of them for his encouragement. *If that is what happened, it would have to have taken place in the interval from the time Paul and Barnabas came there on their first missionary journey till this time we are reading of now in Acts sixteen.* We do know that Judaizers had been there, but seeing their zeal to follow Paul around and contradict his message we are not surprised by that. We also know that prophets in the early church travelled in teams. Two were sent from Jerusalem to Antioch (Acts 15:32-33). But from Jerusalem to Antioch is not

70

the same as from Jerusalem to Galatia. Those three churches were quite far off of the usual circuit. It is not impossible, but not probable that prophets or any other of the five-fold ministry had travelled through during that time.

Either way we consider it, I can only picture it being a gathering of leaders *who normally labor in that geographic area.* The concept is developed from a presbytery in the Jewish nation. It was an official council or board of "elders." It was not a gathering for one occasion or an impromptu assembly which ceased to have the identity of "presbytery" after the prophecies were delivered. Now certainly some of those "elders" could have prophetic giftings or even be emerging prophets. But the point is, they were not strangers to the ones they ministered to.

The presbyters who laid hands on Timothy must have known him well. This is not to say that it would not be good, or *even advantageous* to have visiting prophets minister in these meetings. Silas—a recognized prophet in the early church—was with Paul on this visit to the Galatian churches and probably was meeting Timothy for the first time. No doubt he was in the presbytery meeting. The thing to glean in all of this is a comprehension of who the presbyters really were. The emphasis of the early church presbytery was not upon the prophetic office, but upon the "elders" from a group of churches who had something in common that made it right to be this "council" or "board". I think we need to rediscover the idea of who the presbyters were and the vital role they had in speaking into the lives of those they laid hands on. Let me illustrate from the ministry of the high priest of Israel.

In the next chapter I will discuss the use of the Urim and Thumim as part of the high priest's articles for officiating in his office. Basically what we will see is that by means of these articles God revealed in a supernatural way His will for the nation. But this was not extensive revelation. In its "supernaturalness" it was similar to the revelation that prophets received. But it was dissimilar in that it only operated in the context of things that directly related to the sphere of the high priest's oversight. The prophets, on the other hand, received revelation about other nations and many things in God's overall program of redemption. This means that these two articles had special function for overseers that depended not so much on a gifting, but upon the functions of their office to oversee the sheep they were responsible for. Whereas the prophets were *gifted* to receive revelation. Their revelation covered the same spheres as the Urim and Thumim, as well as other things.

It is interesting that, in the beginning when God instituted His way of guidance for the nation, the prophetic office as we are discussing it now was relatively unknown. The Patriarchs were called prophets, and certainly Moses was, too. But it was especially from Samuel on that the prophet's office was really established as in "institution" in the nation. (Acts 3:24). Before that time the normal procedure was for the civil leader to come to the high priest to inquire of the Lord. This was practiced from the time of Joshua up till the time of the kings (Numbers 27:21; I Samuel 14:36-37). However, eventually we find the kings (even the "good" ones) not inquiring of the Lord through the priests, but through the prophets. I cannot say positively why this happened. Going through the priest required a ritual which the kings may have felt too time consuming. We do know that the circumstance of God raising Samuel up in the prophetic office was a declining priesthood. Whatever the reason, the prophetic office "displaced" the use of Urim and Thumim.

In the way that presbyteries are set up today to get a word from the Lord, I wonder if a similar thing has not happened. This is in no way intended to demean the prophets. On the contrary, as I have said, I consider it advantageous for them to be a part of a gathering for that purpose. But we are concerned with getting a clear picture of the early church's concept of presbytery. If we will put the focus not on the prophets, but on the presbyters who have some common area of responsibility toward those receiving the ministry—I see an opportunity for the church to recover the use of Urim and Thumim. Not only in the episcopate of the local church, but in the sphere of presbytery, I see an opportunity for God to reveal His will for those sheep in a precise way. What a marvelous prospect that is!

The other way I see presbytery being practiced today is not centered around the purpose of getting prophetic words (like we have just discussed it), but with a broader purpose of brethren in a certain geographic area coming together in their ministerial roles. In this practice I suppose there is more variety as to why a gathering like that is regarded as a presbytery. Probably the core of the group is a senior brother who has been instrumental as an apostle or "father" in help-ing some of those brethren come forth in their callings. Possibly there will be other ministers present from that same region who are "independent" but find an affinity with the rest of those brethren and a respect for that senior brother. Thus, in this sense the common bond is the senior brother (or brothers).

Another underlying reason for ministers coming together may not center around senior leaders at all, but just regional considerations—ministers in a certain area feeling a need to come together to strengthen one another. However, in that regard there are innumerable ministerial gatherings across the nation. Some of these are broad enough to include mini-sters of a wide spectrum of belief and practice. I think that in most of those cases they would not think of themselves as a presbytery, but rather just as a ministerial gathering functioning on the premise of mutual respect for one another and a willingness to avoid the areas of their differences. The ones who regard themselves as "more" than a mutually-respecting-one-another ministerial group usually have a greater sense of common destiny. They are not coming together just for regional commonness, but have a similar vision; maybe most of them are from the same historical "stream".

I sense that there are two premises that brethren in these gatherings instinctively adhere to. The one premise is that presbyteries in the early church must have constituted some kind of authority. One writer in the post-apostolic era says "The presbytery is to be obeyed as the apostles." Inherent in the concept of presbytery is some expression of government, yet none of us can be emphatic as to exactly what that is for lack of clear scriptural teaching. And the other premise is that presbytery does not conflict with or displace the expressions of episcopate as we have described it thus far (e.g. local church eldership, bishops, and apostolic overseers). We instinctively know this to be true and for that reason feel secure to keep pursuing the idea until the Holy Spirit restores fully to our understanding the meaning of the concept. Indeed, we must pursue it on that premise and anticipate that it serves some "extra" purpose besides over-seeing churches.

Recall the things we said in chapter nine about the nature of that gathering of five ministers at Antioch. That grouping of ministers as such in no way constituted an oversight toward that local church. Their main business was to be an instrument for seeing ministry thrust forth to regions beyond. In Timothy's case presbytery served a similar purpose. It was instrumental in seeing this brother emerge from within the sphere of local church ministry into a trans-local role.

To me, it is safe not to think of presbytery in terms of being another form of government over the churches those presbyters are locally involved in. What business, or concerns of oversight of churches that are not already taken care of by the role of apostles and bishops could justify the need for presbyteries? Had the presbytery Paul referred to come into existence in the twilight years of his ministry, we might conclude that he is making provision for the time the apostles would pass off the scene. In other words, that it was going to replace some (or all) of the apostolic role of overseeing churches on a higher level of administration. But that is not the picture. Presbytery was instituted when apostolic overseeing was prevalent. We must look for other reasons. To help "Timothys" emerge and be presented to a "Paul" is one apparent reason for that first presbytery. I cannot say that is the only reason for the existence of presbyteries, but I can say that helping these "Timothys" get trained and thrust forth is too big of a task for most local churches.

One more point of consideration in comparing the five at Antioch with the presbytery in Galatia. For one thing, they were all in the five-fold ministry. Secondly, it does not appear that there needs to be a structure authority for that kind of gathering to fulfil its function. They were all peers and all on their faces before God! There was a seriousness in their businesses, but a simplicity in the way they related. In the case of the presbytery, there is no reason to expect that its membership was based upon Ephesians 4:11 calling. On the contrary, the emphasis is upon overseeing, not ministry. Whether these presbyters were all the elders from each of the churches involved in that presbytery, or a representative number, I cannot say. Moreover, if Paul considered himself an integral part of the presbytery, that suggests an infrastructure. Paul was the overseeing apostle and had a relationship with the eldership of those three churches. But I suspect that presbytery was more of a regional concern and carried on whether Paul was there or not. Their relationship with Paul would give them a common bond and similar vision, but I am not so sure that Paul's presence there was essential to the concept.

In conclusion, for lack of enough scripture we obviously are forced to look at this subject in a somewhat speculative way. Yet, seeing the importance Paul attaches to it, we must pursue it to the best of our understanding in humble dependence upon the Holy Spirit to guide us. As long as God is working with us, let us continue with confidence the presbyteries which are put together to get a word form the Lord. As long as God puts His stamp of approval upon it, let ministers come together in their respective region to be a presbytery. But at the same time, let us keep before us some guidelines of what appears to have defined the presbytery of the early church. A presbytery was not an occasional gathering of ministers just to get words of prophecy, but a "council of elders" that had an ongoing purpose in gathering. A presbytery was not centered around the prophetic office, but realized that revelatory potential of "elders" giving themselves to the functions of their oversight (We will elaborate upon this in the next chapter). A "council of elders" was in some sense an expression of government outside of the sphere of local church autonomy, and yet not displacing the regular function of bishops and overseeing apostles. Indeed, may God grant us a restoration of all that is embodied in the concept of presbytery.

CHAPTER 12

FOR EDIFICATION

"For though I should boast somewhat more of our authority, which the Lord has given us for edification, and not for destruction, I should not be ashamed" (II Corinthians 10:8).

After the struggles the Church has been through, especially those who were a part of the Charismatic Renewal in the seventies, it is hard for us to associate "edification" and "authority" together. Nevertheless, the authority which God has ordained for the Church *does* pertain to our edification. We cannot expect to be truly built up in the faith without placing ourselves under the authority the Lord has placed in the church. I realize that sincere sheep have been frustrated (and wounded) in this submission because of over-zealous (and sometimes wrongly motivated) ministers. Consequently, my main burden in this writing is to appeal to leaders. It is required of us to show ourselves worthy of this stewardship. In the words of Paul,

"Giving no offense in any thing, that the ministry be not blamed: But in all things approving ourselves as the ministers of God..." (II Corinthians 6:3-4).

Let us consider the diaconate first.

The five-fold ministry experience their authority *according to the word of God*. Primarily this is realized from the written word—the logos. These ministers, leaders given trans-locally to the Church, can speak with boldness and conviction to saints according to the standard of the Scriptures. When the preaching and teaching of these men is according to the Scriptures, God will stand with them and confirm what they say. To illustrate this, if an evangelist, or any ministry came to a congregation and found that believers were marrying unbelievers, he could reasonably feel a compulsion of the Holy Spirit to address the problem. With conviction he could exhort and challenge the church telling them that husbands and wives are to be heirs together of the grace of life and that it is not right for believers to be unequally yoked with unbelievers. Likewise, any of the five-fold ministry could feel a measure of authority in a situation like that. Thus, let us ask ourselves what areas of the Christian life should these leaders feel responsibility about.

From the context of Ephesians four I have arrived at four things which seem reasonable for the ministry to be exercised about. It is likely that according to the specialization of each of the five offices, they will feel greater burdens in one area than another. Evangelists will feel more concern about some areas than the teachers. Likewise, pastors will be exercised differently than prophets, and so forth. I make no attempt to match the specialization of each of the offices to these four areas. Rather, it will be sufficient to say that it is seemly for any of the five-fold ministry to feel responsibility to speak into the churches along the lines of any of these four subjects.

Part of the goal for this anointed Body is to come into the unity of the faith. When "faith" is prefixed with the definite article "the", it refers to more than the exercising of trust in the promises of God. *The faith* speaks of creed or doctrines which define our trust in God. Jude is emphatic that this has been historically "once and for all" committed to the Church.

In the very beginning of the Church age the original apostles were vested with a special authority in the word. Like the Old Testament prophets, their words became part of the scriptural canon. Moreover, it also pertained to their ministry to formulate basic doctrines of the faith. Obviously, neither the apostles nor any other of the Ephesians 4:11 ministry carry that kind of authority today. We need neither new doctrines, nor additional books in the sacred canon, but we do need to be kept within the boundaries of orthodox faith. So, the first area of their responsibility concerns *basic doctrines of the faith.*

I have already made reference to the futility of having a church richly gifted to speak, but lacking in moral character. The "mature man" that Paul envisions is more than a Body trained and experienced in all five of those anointings. There must be moral excellence. We are to grow up *in all aspects* into Him,.." When sin and worldliness come into the Church, it is reasonable for the ministry to feel an authority to counter this. Thus, the second area of their responsibility concerns *moral standards.*

The third area of their concern is *the mission of the church.* The saints are being equipped "for the work of service." The focus of the context is on the internal life of the Body and how it mutually interacts, but it is not limited to that. The service is also external. The Church is to express Christ to a needy world, but how? Is our mission to get our man into the White House? Are we to give ourselves only to social actions? Are we to preach the gospel only and ignore social problems? What is our direction? We need the ministry to keep us on course.

The fourth area concerns *the pattern and order for the church life.* To speak of a mature man certainly implies orderliness and design. Paul seems to strain for words to describe the marvelous way the parts are fitted and held together. Not only are the members beautifully joined to one another, but together they are joined to the Head. This fitting and joining allows for full expression of both *life* and *government* in this mature man. Lest we degenerate into a religious system or a social club, we need the ministry to exhort us and guide us to our goal. Let us turn our thoughts now to the episcopate.

According to their ministerial ability in preaching and teaching, overseers also would have authority according to the Word. But besides that, there is a dimension of authority which naturally follows their shepherding relationship *with those particular sheep*. Recall the things which were said in Chapter Five concerning feeding. Our tendency in "learning" is to focus on receiving information without necessarily being really committed to letting it change our lives. Real true feeding involves discipline. The rod and staff of the shepherd is not only for bringing protection from wolves. It also brings correction to the sheep. (Psalm 23:4) I fear that we have focused so much on the disseminating of information that we have lost sight of the way the shepherd's rod is inherent in the meaning of "feed". But we are reminded in the extreme by the description of the Son of God who will one day return to "feed" the nations with a rod of iron (Revelation 12:5; 19:15)!

Exactly what is this dimension of authority that is unique to the role of overseers? The Chief Shepherd has not only prescribed general standards for all His sheep, He also has a specific will for each of their lives. If overseers faithfully give themselves to the function of their role, God will reveal in some measure His will for those particular sheep. To the extent that God reveals this to those who are overseeing, to that extent there is a commensurate authority for them to guide those sheep into that will. Let me illustrate how this works by using the example of the high priest of Israel (Exodus 28:15-30).

Part of the high priest's attire was a breastpiece on which were twelve stones representing each of the twelve tribes. This would describe the area of his responsibility, his oversight. Whenever he came before the Lord in intercession, he bore them upon his heart. Inside the breastpiece there was a kind of pocket where the Urim and Thummim were placed. We do not know much about these two curious articles except that they were means of God revealing His will for the nation. The significant thing is the relationship of the Urim and Thummim to the breastpiece. It was in the context of that bishopric and through the means of intercession that those two articles "worked" to reveal God's will. It will be no less so today when overseers maintain a meaningful involvement with the sheep and give themselves to travailing prayer for them. The Chief Shepherd will reveal His will. Thus we can say that overseers experience their authority *according to the revealed will of God.*

I used the example of an evangelist coming to a church and finding believers marrying unbelievers. Now suppose that there is a brother and sister who wish to get married. As far as the standard of the written word is concerned, this is appropriate. But what about God's will for their lives individually? Possibly God has made it known to those elders that the young man is called to serve God overseas in very difficult areas and that the sister is not called to share that kind of life. If the Lord has really revealed that, it is very appropriate for them to feel authority to challenge their plans—to reprove and exhort them with much patience. Obviously we are looking now at a serious kind of authority.

Possibly we can say that the greatest hurts, the greatest abuses relating to authority have occurred in the roles of the episcopate more than the diaconate. When overseers presume to know God's will for sheep, in areas where the Chief Shepherd really has not revealed it, there is abuse. Or when it is revealed, but authority is not administered in a

81

Christ-like way, it hurts! Then we are transgressing in those areas where we are not to lord it over them, or over their faith (I Peter 5:3; II Corinthians 1:24). Thus far we have discussed the measure of the rule as being limited in the sense of which ones are affected by it. Let us remind ourselves that it is also limited in the extent that it touches those particular sheep affected by it. There is only One with unlimited authority. Truly, those who are going to express this rule must fear the Lord, be of a humble heart, and have much love and wisdom!

For the remainder of this chapter, I want to turn from talking about shepherds and appeal to the sheep. We do not want to lose the impetus of the good things of the Charismatic or other renewal movements. The Holy Spirit is brooding over the Church, deeply yearning to see every member equipped, mobilized, and launched into ministry. We can only speculate as to how wonderful it will be when that Body is mature, when there is a rich deposit of all five anointings distributed among the members, when we reach that "until" (Ephesians 4:13). What will happen to the five-fold ministry at that time? Are they literally no longer given in the sense that they are not among us? I think it will be something like the times in the Old Testament when the glory of the Lord filled the Tabernacle or the Temple and the priests could not enter in to perform their usual duties. There have been occasions during the Church age when God came down in awesome visitations. At times like that it does not seem to matter whether there are men to lead or not. However, those visitations could not be sustained for long and eventually it was necessary that Christ have his appointed leaders on the scene. It is one thing for the risen Christ to fill the church with His glory and to put His restraints upon the ministry at that time. It is quite another thing for saints to be idealistic and to suppose that negating the role of the ministry will "produce" the glory. Without dampening our zeal to seek Him for His fullness, let us not be found embracing an idealism which borders on anarchy. God cannot honor anarchy! Regardless of the problems of the past and whatever hope we entertain for the future, we cannot at this time expect to be without His government as expressed through His appointed men. He has ordained that authority for our edification.

CHAPTER 13

QUALIFICATIONS FOR ELDERS

So far our study has concerned itself with the principles by which God works to bring about His government in the church. Also, various forms in which this government is expressed were considered. I have endeavored to do this by addressing the three forms of lawlessness mentioned in Chapter One. In Chapter Seven we dealt with the mistake of trying to rule the church with a concept of co-equal type eldership. And in the last chapter I appealed to those who feel that they need only to submit directly to the Lord and not the leaders He places in the church. Now we are turning our thoughts from principles, concepts, and forms to consider the men who do the leading. No matter how much success we attain comprehending and setting in place the principles for governing the church, *that government would still be no better than the men in those places of responsibility.* Therefore, to address the problem of usurpation, let us conclude this study by talking about the qualifications for leaders. We will look first at those who are in the Ephesians 4:11 ministry.

When these men are ready to be recognized and placed into the ministry, there are three areas that come into consideration. The first area is *character*. For those who are overseers there are lists of character qualities to define their role, but I do not know that we can find such a well-defined standard to describe those who are called to preach. This should not surprise us since overseeing, by the very nature of its work, requires them to be involved with the sheep. Whether it be bishops like Timothy and Titus (I Timothy 4:12; Titus 2:7-8), or elders in a local church (I Peter 5:3), leading by example is basic to the way overseers influence the sheep. Conversely, it means that their lives are under close examination—more so, perhaps, than those who are given trans-locally to serve the Body of Christ. Indeed, it would appear that preachers with flawed character, but real giftedness in their office can gain acceptance and have their role in equipping the saints while overseers are being held to a stricter accountability! Suffice it to say, it is serious business for ministers to presume upon the long-suffering of God and His graciousness in giving gifts irrevocably. Those who preach the gospel should take their calling seriously and seek to have the nine-fold fruit of the Spirit formed in them.

The second area of recognition is *gifting*. We are not thinking so much of the nine manifestations of the Spirit (I Corinthians 12:8-10). Those are like tools of the trade and enhance the effectiveness of the ministry. Primarily we are thinking of the office itself being a gift. In chapter two we attempted to show that the Spirit's goal is to give a rich deposit of all five anointings in the entire Body. That would mean that brothers and sisters could expect that their Acts 1:8 anointing would manifest characteristics of one (or more) of the anointings of those five offices. It remains to be seen how rich that distribution in the Body is going to be! But does an anointing of one of those offices really constitute being in the office itself? What is it in the gifting of these Ephesians 4:11 men that distinguishes them from the rest?

Primarily this gifting manifests itself in an ability to receive messages directly from God and proclaim them to the people. The Lord commended Peter for being able to have it revealed directly to him from the Father (Matthew 16:17). To establish his rank with the other apostles, Paul made it clear that he did not get his message second-hand, but directly from God (Galatians 1:11-12,16; 2:6). This should not make us unappreciative of the process of learning second-hand. Nor should we forget the faithfulness of the Holy Spirit to bear witness to truth and teach every believer. But the operation is not quite the same as what we are considering here. It just seems that God has reserved the method of direct revelation as a way of singling out those He places in authority. And the more direct the revelation, the greater the authority (Numbers 11:6-8).

Every believer who yields to the Lord is going to have personal instruction from the Word. And from the things the Lord directly shows him and from what he is taught, there is a blessing when he testifies by the anointing of the Spirit. But that "blessing" just is not the same as what we observe when one of these called-ones share what they have received. There is something "extra" that we can discern when they speak. There is an awareness that God is with them and singling them out to be a preacher of the gospel. It truly is a gift of God. And as this gift manifests itself in the earliest stages, there is not much specialization. But eventually that gift will manifest itself in one or more of the Ephesians 4:11 offices. For men to be accepted as those given trans-locally and yet not be in possession of this gift would be a mistake.

The third thing is that there is developed in them *a body of truth* or, we might say *theology*. No minister can expect to be effective that does not have a working knowledge of the Bible and comprehension of basic doctrines of the faith (II Timothy 2:15; 3:16-17). Without this, we are ill-prepared! We must realize that this third thing is not inherent in the gifting we just spoke of; there is no substitute for diligent, disciplined study of the Word of God. It is so important that we make the distinction between the *gift* and *acquired knowledge* of the truth. There are some men who are formally trained in theology, but do not have the gift. However sincere they may be, this inadequacy will manifest itself in their ministry. On the other hand, there are those who truly posses the gift, but for whatever reason have not given themselves to a learning process. They may get by for awhile, but eventually this lack is going to show up in their ministry.

There are other things we may wish to see in those who minister the word, but we must be careful that we are not requiring something that God does not require. He puts His treasures in earthen vessels. He seems to deliberately choose men with flawed humanity and to require of us to look beyond the "earthiness" and see the treasure. Even in the three points we discussed, they are relative standards. How much the Lord requires them to qualify in each point to some extent will be determined by the role He has planned for them. Before their own Master and according to the plan He has for their life, they will either stand of fall (Romans 14:4). However, when it comes to the episcopate, the requirements are clearer, and in some ways stricter.

First of all, there are the *character* qualifications. As I said, these leaders influence by their example.

"Remember those who led you, who spoke the word of God to you; and *considering the outcome of their way of life*, imitate their faith." (Hebrews 13:7).

This is important for any who are leaders, but especially for those in oversight roles. For this reason, we are not surprised that Paul is careful to list specific character qualities for this work. In his letters to Timothy and Titus, altogether nineteen things are given for a description of the character of these men.

The second qualification I call *managerial ability*. When God told Moses what to look for in those seventy men, He specified that they were to be elders of the people "and their officers" (Numbers 11:6). These *officers* are first mentioned during the time of Israel's captivity in Egypt (Exodus 5:14-21). The Egyptians selected these men from the ranks of Israel to be overseers for the work assignments. The Egyptians were not concerned with moral excellence or spiritual qualities. They selected these men on the basis of ability which was observable in them—ability to manage people. It is this ability that Paul has in mind when he says, **"He must be one who manages his own household well, keeping his children under control with all dignity..." (I Timothy 3:4).** Overseers must have a broad perspective and not be given to tangents or peripheral issues. Of necessity there has to be a certain amount of business meetings to communicate and coordinate activities. To a certain extent techniques of management can be acquired through training, but more basic to this is whether or not they have a capacity of soul for this work. There must be a certain capacity of emotion, intellect, and will to take hold of administrative duties. Men without this capacity who attempt to rule will find it tedious and burdensome, and eventually will experience vexations to the point of losing that "dignity."

The third qualification I refer to as *ministerial ability* in the word of God. Feeding sheep is basic to the work of overseeing. Those who do this must have a certain comprehension of basic doctrines and some persuasiveness in their exhorting. Paul tells Timothy that elders must be able to teach, but how much ability is that (I Timothy 3:2)? When he states this same requirement to Titus, he says that the overseer is "holding fast the faithful word as he has been taught, that he may be able by sound doctrine both to exhort, and to convince the gainsayers" (Titus 1:9). This does not describe the kind of giftedness the five-fold ministry have who can receive directly from God. These elders are good students who have been well taught. Neither does it portray them necessarily as giving sermons, or being the main source through whom the flock is taught. Rather, they are portrayed as those who are watching and who correct others who are speaking (e.g. the gainsayers).

In each of these three is there an absolute standard that will satisfy the requirements of what all overseers are to be? The Lord said,

> **"From everyone who has been given much shall much be required; and to whom they entrusted much, of him they will ask all the more" (Luke 12:48).**

It will be required at the end of the race when the stewards stand before the Master and give an account. But it is also required of them now by those who follow them.

I realize that when lawless influences are working in the hearts of people, they can have unrealistic expectations for their leaders. Dismissing that for the moment, we are considering the realistic expectations which God puts in their hearts to desire from those who lead them. How much is that? I think the expectation and the requirements are in proportion to the degree of the role. Concerning managerial ability, the very minimum would be for a man to have the capacity to control his own family. However, to "control" a group of churches would obviously require greater ability. It is likewise for ministerial ability. It is one thing on the local church level to have "holding fast" elders who are watching and keeping things in right boundaries. Hopefully, among them there will be some elders who are in one of the ministry offices. But on the bishop level I do not think this is optional. I do not see how churches can be cared for by an extra-local overseer if he does not have the ministerial ability of Ephesians 4:11.

Character qualifications is a delicate issue today. But in this point also the requirements are in proportion to the greatness of the stewardship. For example, in the matter of divorce and remarriage, Israel had three standards. For the congregation, they were permitted to divorce and remarry under certain circumstances. However, priests could not marry a woman who was not a virgin, or who had been divorced. They could possibly marry a foreigner who was not an idolater or a Canaanite, or they could marry a widow of irreproachable character. The high priest could not marry a woman who was not a virgin, who had been divorced, or who is a widow. He could only marry a virgin Israelite (Leviticus 21:13-14)! I am not suggesting that we are supposed to take literally each of these points and impose them in the church. But in principle it should alert us to the fact that we cannot arrive at one standard that will satisfy the requirements for *all* overseers. What may be a good standard for elders in the local church may not be strict enough to define the standard for bishops or apostles.

We will take one more chapter to talk about qualifications for leaders, but I want to conclude this chapter with remarks about lawlessness. I have especially addressed my remarks to the problem of usurpation—the wrong men being in the right positions. Usurpation is a strong word and suggests bad character. However, I have discussed more than bad character. There are many cases of faithful men with a good heart who have volunteered and come into roles of leadership which in the process of time manifest their inability. Consider the evangelist who is truly anointed in his preaching and has a pure heart, but really has no capacity to manage people. Were he to begin, for whatever reason to try to oversee some of the fruits of his ministry, it would frustrate those who have been blessed by him. Proverbs says that it is unbecoming, and unsettling for those who do not have managerial ability to come into those positions (Proverbs 30:21-

22; 19:10). But on the other hand, what often happens is that men who do not have this capacity, men who are natural born leaders—get saved and too quickly are given places of leadership. There has not been enough time to really prove their character. This is the case that does the greatest harm to the cause of Christ. This is most unbecoming case of all (Proverbs 26:1, Ecclesiastes 10:5-6). Therefore, let us be knowledgeable of all the things that describe qualified leadership and seek to get the right men into the right positions. Most of all let us be wary of men of bad character getting into those places.

CHAPTER **14**

WOMEN IN MINISTRY

To complete our study of qualifications for leadership, we need to look at of the role of women. Needless to say, women in leadership has become a sensitive subject, but it needs to be addressed. We will develop our thoughts by first considering the prospect of their having roles in the episcopate, and then by considering the possibility of the diaconate.

Those who have championed the cause of greater expressions for women usually point to Galatians 3:26-28,

> **"For you are all sons of God through faith in Christ Jesus. For all of you who were baptized into Christ have clothed yourselves with Christ. There is neither Jew nor Greek, there is neither slave nor free man, there is neither male nor female; for you are all one in Christ Jesus."**

This text might be applicable if Paul were dealing with church order here, but he is not. The passage that does deal with this issue in relation to church order is Paul's first letter to Timothy (see I Timothy 2:8-15). This letter is the apostle's instruction to this young bishop on how things should be ordered in church life (e.g. "how one ought to behave in the household of God" (I Timothy 3:15). In this passage he intentionally raises the question of two specific issues: (1) The matter of women being in authority, and (2) the matter of women teaching in public meetings. It cannot be asserted that this one passage alone is a balanced statement of *all* roles of women serving in church life. Nevertheless, it is a key passage and will suffice for most of what I will say in this writing.

The two central verses are eleven and twelve where four important words are used. The woman is to receive instruction with entire *submissiveness*. This word is related to the one where Paul tells wives to be subject to their husbands in all things (Ephesians 5:24). Submission or subordination primarily describes a way of relating to another person. It includes a disposition to respond to authority. The second word is found in the phrase where he enjoins them to *quietness* rather than teaching. This is not the same word he uses in I Corinthians 14:33; a word which means that in some situations women are to make no sound at all. Rather the quietness here speaks of an attitude—calmness and peace. The thought well comes out in Paul's instruction to saints in Macedonia when he tells them to "make it your ambition to lead a quiet life and attend to your own business..." (1 Thessalonians 4:11). The thought is to be concerned with one's own affairs, and not trying to handle something outside one's sphere of responsibility. In other words, he is not saying for women to refrain from all speech in the assembly, but speech in accordance with the guidelines he is giving here.

The third word is *teach*. I fear that the influence of modern education has hindered us from understanding the early church's concept of teaching. To be taught today implies that a person has intellectually grasped the information. It has nothing to do with his own personal commitment to the subject. Nor does the method of being taught require him to be committed to his instructor. Basically the teacher today is one who disseminates information. But in the practice of the early church the teacher does not merely give his views of the subject, he expects the student to act upon them. The teaching process occurred within a structured relationship between the instructor and the pupil. The pupil regarded the teacher as being in authority over his life. In other words, teaching was regarded as an expression of authority.

The fourth word could best be translated *have authority*. Unfortunately, this is the only occurrence of this word in the New Testament, and it never appears in the Septuagint. Consequently, there is some debate regarding the precise meaning. The three possible meanings usually held by translators are: To have authority, to usurp authority, or to domineer. When we consider the ramifications of these three, it comes down to two ideas. Either Paul intends it to be a prohibition against all ruling of women over men, or, it infers that under proper circumstances women can rule over men. I will give three reasons why I think it is a prohibition of women ruling over men under any circumstance.

Some have suggested that there were certain classes of women in the churches that Timothy had to contend with. Perhaps some wealthy women who came into the faith tended to carry their social status with them and were assertive in Christian gatherings. Or perhaps women who hosted assemblies in their homes felt they had a right to govern the proceedings of the meeting. There is nothing in the context that suggests that Paul is addressing certain *kinds* of women. Secondly, if wrong use of authority was the only issue, there is no reason for him to single out the sisters. Obviously men also are guilty of doing it wrong. Thirdly, Paul substantiates his teaching by referring back to the original order with Adam and Eve. This indicates that the problem concerns the fact that women are over men, not merely that they are doing it wrong.

Paul's reference to the creation pattern arouses all manner of ideas on this subject. It encourages, on the one hand those who seem to wish to put the sisters down and treat them as inferior citizens of the kingdom of God. On the other hand, those who defend the sisters react and see in these verses reason to call Paul a male chauvinist. We must be careful to not weaken the meaning of sacred scripture by looking too much at what we may think the humanity of God's servants to be. Those who presume that Paul *may* have had an unhappy marriage and he *may* have been tempted to be unnecessarily strict in his views of women (Ecclesiastes 7:27-28), have no Biblical or historical evidence on which to base such conclusions on, and it is beside the point. When God selects His vessels, He is thoroughly aware of their flaws and is well able to move through them and cause them to say what He wants them to say *in spite of their personal views*. It was not an accident or coincidence that God chose this man to give us teaching on the order for church life. Paul was inspired by the Spirit when addressing this issue and we should receive his words as Holy Writ (I Corinthians 14:37-38).

Let no one suppose that Paul is trying to blame women for plunging the human race into sin. If one is responsible, it is man (Romans 5:12). Neither should we interpret this subject from the prohibition the Lord God spoke to the woman *after* the Fall. If that is Paul's intent, then rightly so it could be said that those restrictions on the women's role are altered through redemption. In his explanation of the man being created first, he is clearly referring to something prior to the Fall to substantiate his view. And neither should men think that Paul is making a statement about an inherent weakness of all women—that is, that women are more deceivable than men. That is not his intent. If that were his point, then it could be reasonably argued that in redemption the sisters weaknesses are overcome and they can qualify for governing roles.

Paul sees in the Adam and Eve event a type, and nothing more. Let us not read into his analysis something that is not there. Man and woman have complementary roles which are demonstrated both in the Fall and in redemption. God's plan is not to save the human race apart from the woman (I Corinthians 11:11), but to save it with the Savior born of a woman (Galatians 4:40). But in the outworking of those complementary roles, God has ordained an order for the life of the redeemed community—an order illustrated in the first pair. Since the first man and woman acted out their roles in the fashion they did, Paul sees in that a precedence for what is to follow.

I must conclude that in the general assembly of believers which involve men and women, it is inappropriate for women to be in governmental roles. Certainly ministry to women only, or ministry to children do not have these restrictions. Moreover, we do have situations today where "teaching" is fitted to a different mode. If it is catechism classes or something aimed at disseminating information, why would anyone find it objectionable for women to do this? But if it is "teaching" in the mode of a master making disciples, the prohibition is clear.

If women are not to be in the episcopate, what about the diaconate? Would the limited form of "teaching" I just described preclude the possibility of sisters being in the five-fold ministry? One is hard pressed to find even one clear example in the early church of a sister who is acknowledged in a singular way as being in the ministry! Some have tried to make much of the Junias whom Paul mentions as being well-known among the apostles, but it is not clear that this is a husband-wife combination (Romans 16:7). The RSV translation refers to them as "men". If they are a couple, it still is not an example of singularness, but of a special combination. It would be like Priscilla and Aquila who instructed Apollos (Acts 18:26). It is conceivable that she was not only gifted as a teacher, but *more gifted* than Aquila. Nevertheless, in the outworking of those giftings, she did not aspire to work in a singular way, nor was there an arrangement where the husband was in a supporting role of "her ministry". Rather, their giftings were blended to express the husband-wife roles in a way that agrees with God's order.

In the case of single sisters, be they unmarried, widowed, or possibly divorced, there are examples of them working with teams. A quote from the writings of Clement of Alexandria illustrates the practice in the beginning of Christianity. "The apostles, giving themselves without respite to the work of evangelism, as befitted their ministry took with them women, not as wives but as sisters, to share in their ministry to women living at home: by their agency the teaching of the Lord reached the womens' quarters without arousing suspicion." And we know that Paul included sisters on his teams (Romans 16:1-7; Philippians 4:2-3). Yet, we have no examples of sisters leading those teams and no examples of them with the appellation of "apostles" or any other of the Ephesians 4:11 ministry.

The best way I can illustrate this is to refer to the occasion when Paul was visiting Philip (Acts 21:8-14). Two things impress me in Luke's account. First of all, he does not use terms loosely, but is rather precise in the way he identifies things. He does not refer to the four daughters as prophetesses, but as those who prophesy. Yet, he identifies their father as "the evangelist" and Agabus as "the prophet". Not only here, but throughout Acts he makes these recognitions of office. And the second thing is the silence concerning the content of the prophesies of those four daughters. Luke's purpose in writing Acts was to present a defense to the Roman government for Paul's being a controversial figure. Anything that contributed to Paul's decision to go to Jerusalem should have been included in the account. Agabus' prophecy is recorded. It would significantly influence Paul's decision on the trip. I must assume that if the prophecies of the daughters were not recorded, it is because their messages were not governmental or directional. They were of a different nature—a nature befitting the role of sisters speaking into the life of a minister of Christ. Thus, using this account as an illustration, I want to make three observations.

First of all, properly identifying a ministerial role does not answer all the questions. It is wonderful to me that Luke could name things so clearly. In doing so, he not only recognizes that that person is in the Ephesians 4:11 office, but which one he is in! We are not very clear today in some cases. For example, at what point is a brother in the office of prophet and not merely a prophetic brother? Or when do ministers who are apostolic become apostles? Despite the awkwardness we feel sometimes in identifying which ministry a person is in, usually we can have a sense that they are at least in the category of Ephesians 4:11. We can have a sense of them reaching a level of maturity and experience that makes it appropriate to send them forth trans-locally; appropriate to acknowledge them in a singular way as being in the diaconate. But what about the sisters? If we *do give* them the titles of those five offices, would that be saying that they are given trans-locally in a singular fashion; are they "given" to the Church the same as the brother in those offices?

Furthermore, we must remember that other writers were not as precise as Luke, and they were not attempting to identify things in the manner we are discussing. When the Spirit came upon the seventy, Moses' response was "Would that all the Lord's people were prophets, that the Lord would put His Spirit upon them!" (Numbers 11:29). The inference of this statement is that now seventy Israelites are "prophets" and Moses wished that it were so of them all. Does he actually mean "prophet" in the sense that they would be in that Old Testament office like Isaiah, Jonah and the rest? Or does he not simply mean in the sense that the Spirit comes upon them and they prophesy? An example of an even more liberal application of terminology is where the wife of Isaiah is referred to as "the prophetess" (Isaiah 8:3). There is nothing to suggest that she was in the office, or that she is being identified for an anointing along those lines. It appears she is called that only because she is his wife. If we are going to use such references we must be careful to use them according to the context and Biblical intent.

Secondly, the anointing and giftings which correspond to one of the offices does not constitute the office itself. God's calling for Israel is that they will be a whole nation of priests! Thus far they have come short. Yet the prophets spoke of a future Israel that does attain, (Isaiah 61:4-6). However, in that glorified Israel where the ministerial experience of the whole nation excels, it does not do so in a manner that obliterates the distinction of the ordained priestly office (Isaiah 66:21).

Also, I imagine that Moses' statement was more than a wish, but a vision he cherished for Israel to become a prophetic nation. When a future Israel does experience Joel's promise, does it mean that those sons and daughters are in the prophetic office (Joel 2:28-29)? It is likewise for that anointed Body of Christ of which we have said so much. When anointings corresponding to each of the five offices are richly distributed on our sons and daughters, does it mean they have been placed in those offices? It is conceivable to me that at that time some of them will have even richer anointings than do some evangelists and teachers at this present time simply because of the intensity of the visitation in that hour!

According to one contemporary writer Philip's four daughters were noted for their anointing in a way that classified them with Silas, Agabus, and the other prophets. It would be foolish for anyone to deny that there are women with rich anointings and giftings of these offices—in some cases greater than men. Moreover, no one can deny God the prerogative to raise up women in a singular way and work with them in a fashion that would appear to be the exception to His way. However, while making allowance for exceptions and being appreciative of giftings invested in women, we must make it our task to define the normal order—an order which we can substantiate it from the Word.

The third observation is similar to the second. When Christ gives gifts to people, He does not grant with it a carte blanche for using it. Stated another way, God leaves it up to us to find the proper order for using those gifts. It is amazing how God can apparently bless the gifts, bless the anointing and yet possibly be displeased with areas of our life which we may consider not directly related to our ministry. This can be illustrated in the way Moses was commissioned to go back down into Egypt. When we read that encounter we get the distinct impression that God was approving His servant and that the only thing wrong was that Moses was dragging his feet. But after he is commissioned and on his way, God confronts him about an area of his life that was not even discussed during the encounter. The Lord was actually ready to kill him, and it seems would have had not his wife used wisdom and intervened! (Exodus 4:24-26). Bear in mind the issue was not merely one act of disobedience. The disobedience was manifestation of a deeper problem—disorder in the home life. Moses was not really taking his role as head of his household. What a sobering example!

It appears that in many cases, in the beginning of their ministries, God does not make it an issue in the lives of his servants like he did with Moses. God's dealings may come years later after they are launched into a successful public ministry. What a temptation to interpret that "success" as a sign of God's approval of all we are doing! Not only that, it would seem that sometimes God is not so confrontational as that and, so to speak, does not make an issue of it. Even that should not be construed as His best. Brothers or sisters serving the Lord—we should take seriously the matter of doing things God's way. Whether He chooses to make an issue of it, or whether the Holy Spirit gently strives with us about it, one thing is for sure: We cannot expect to violate God's order and not experience that adverse effect of it. Somewhere down the line it will affect the fruit of our ministry.

Regarding the diaconate, I want to conclude with one last consideration. Whether we decide to call the gifted women "evangelist" or "prophetess", etc is not the real issue. The issue is in the application. In what sense are they to be regarded as one "given" trans-locally? How are their giftings going to be expressed in the church life? And just as seriously, how is it going to be expressed publicly in society? Paul says in graphic terms that the ministry is a spectacle. (I Corinthians 4:9). And then in one of his teachings about man/woman relationships in community life, at one point he makes an appeal for us to understand by that which "nature" teaches us (I Corinthians 11:14). I believe what he is saying is that there is something inherent in all societies that causes them to know that there are different roles for men and women.

I would like to illustrate this by referring to the Chinese character for "security". It is composed of two radicals which depict "women" under the "roof". The ancients had the wisdom to know that woman's basic role is a domestic one (Titus 2:4-5) and it was in fulfilling that role that society would know "security", or stability.

I have already mentioned Paul's pointing back to the Adam/Eve arrangement as setting the pace for all societies. My point is, we must be careful about measuring our standards by what may be an acceptable mode for women in American society. We are seeking to know God's basic pattern, His order for His creatures. And whatever that pattern is, I anticipate that it agrees with "nature". It is something that is generally recognizable all over the world. This is important for the church in America for two reasons. First of all, it effects our strategy for communicating the gospel cross-culturally. And secondly, we need to give serious considera-tion to the place society is at in reference to the home, and all that pertains to that. If women are to go public in singular fashion, they must be careful that this is not sending mixed signals to society. The church must posture itself in society in a way that is a challenge to it and that can effect a change in trends that do not foster God's ways. May God grant us much wisdom and grace in these matters.

CHAPTER **15**

UNTIL HE COMES

The prophet Ezekiel looked at the decayed state of things in his generation. One king after another came to power and one after another was removed. There seemed to be nothing stable anywhere in the kingdom. In the visitations of the Spirit he looked into the future and told of the time when the throne would finally be established. As part of that theme he said, "I will overturn, overturn, overturn it: and it shall be no more, until he come whose right it is; and I will give it to him" (Ezekiel 21:27).

In the closing days of His earthy ministry, the Lord Jesus gave a clear word to the sincere people of that generation. He said,

> **"The scribes and the pharisees sit in Moses' seat: All therefore whatsoever they bid you observe, that observe and do; but do not ye after their works; for they say, and do not" (Matthew 23:2-3).**

Truly, "Moses seat" was a system instituted by God for governing Israel. Yet the way religious leaders were ruling in that system was not expressing God's true government for the nation. Be that as it may, the Lord did not "tear down" the system as such, but showed a certain respect for it. He had plenty to say about the *men* in that system, but after saying these things with respect for the system, He went on to prophesy its end.

After the Lord's ascension the church was born. While the old system still remained, Heaven gave birth to a new one! For a season the believers were a part of the old and the new, and God's blessing was mightily upon them. Yet, the Lord intended that the new order would have its own clear, distinct identity apart from the old. How was this transition to come about? I cannot emphatically say. It appears that in some things they were dragging their feet (e.g. the matter of including the Gentiles). On the other hand, I do not get the impression that God was leading them to suddenly come out of Judaism en masse and sever all ties! One thing is sure. In a matter of years, God himself judged the former system with the destruction of the city. The true believers were automatically "out."

In the years that transpired since then, the Church itself has gone through many upheavals. For a while it functioned as a truly spiritual order, and the ruling of Christ was beautifully expressed toward His people. Gradually it degenerated. In some cases the men themselves were corrupt and not qualified to rule. In general, the whole system changed and departed from the original pattern. In the process of time, God sovereignly and graciously visited one of those generations, with the result that many came out of the old order and a new one began. Something new was born from heaven! Once again, whether or not the transition from the old to the new happened just as Christ intended it, only eternity will reveal. The fact is, it did happen. And, without a doubt, succeeding generations of the church profited from the things that people in that visitation experienced.

It is sad to look at the history of the church and see that when a generation is so wonderfully blessed by one of those visitations, it is but a matter of time till the new thing declines!

Will there never be an end to these cycles? However we may interpret all of this, there are two positive things in the picture. It is most encouraging to see that when things *do* decline, the Spirit of God will continue His work and in His own sovereign way, visit again. Praise and glory be unto him who is so faithful! And the other thing we notice is that when succeeding generations loose the vitality of the visitation, the truth remains with us. Each visitation is instrumental in conveying a particular message from God, in restoring understanding of scripture, and that deposit remains with us. I think we take for granted how much we are the beneficiaries of this historical process. No doubt we can say that because of this, in some ways the next visitation is able to begin on a higher plane than the former one. A gradual restoration is progressively taking place in history!

During these cycles, generally speaking, the trend has been for the old order to not be tolerant of the emerging new orders. Misunderstandings and strained feelings forced many of these to come out of their groups whether they really wanted to or not. In some cases, some of those who were blessed were more adventuresome and came out, when in reality they were not being forced out. In the Charismatic Renewal there has been a more tolerant mood. Leaders of various denominations have seen this as an opportunity to revitalize their ranks, and have encouraged charismatic believers to stay. Because of this, many have held a hope for the historical churches, both Protestant and Catholic. Some national leaders have told us that coming out is a thing of the past. Others have persisted to say that God is up to something new.

Some seem to visualize a perfect* church *before* the Lord comes, but I cannot see that. I cannot imagine "perfection"

---

* I use the word "perfect" not in its theological sense (e.g. Matthew 5:48), but in its usage in modern English.

before the Lord comes and puts the finishing touch on things. But on the other hand, I do see a church that is glorious by the time of His advent—a church that is marvelously united which the world can see and recognize as the Body of Christ, in which the authority of Christ can be expressed from the Head to each part of the Body—true spiritual ruling. The church of the first century made a great impact upon its generation. I expect the last-day church to have as great a ministry, if not greater, than the former church. Therefore, although perfection may not be attained, glory will be. The Lord is calling us to a much higher experience than we presently enjoy.

We cannot afford to weaken our vision. When I consider the mission of the church to our generation, and see the increasing pressures of lawlessness, I entertain little hope for existing ecclesiastical systems *as such* to meet the need. I cannot say positively what will happen to each of these systems. I commit that to the Lord. As long as these systems do exist, however, I will do nothing to tear them down, but will show proper respect for them (and love for my brethren within them.) One thing is for sure. Until the church comes into the order the Lord intends for her, He will not rest. We can expect "overturn, overturn, overturn." It is the Lord Jesus' right alone to rule in the Church.

Therefore, for those whom the Lord has not called out of a declining group, do not be dismayed. As long as it is God's will for you to be there, let your light shine without compromise. At the same time, do not lose sight of the ultimate goal which the Lord is bringing us all into. As for those who find themselves "out" of their groups, rejoice. You have an opportunity to practice more freely the principles you see in the Word. Nevertheless, do not forget the lesson of church history. However wonderful the "new" thing is that you move into, God is not obligated to keep working with it (Romans 11:35). If at any point the "right" is taken away from the Lord and given to men, from that time another "over-turn" is on the way. Therefore, wherever we find ourselves today, let us keep our eyes on the Lord and not be surprised when the overturn comes. Let us have great confidence in Him to build His church—a church which He can freely rule.

The Morning Star Journal

For the most up-to-date prophetic messages and insights from this ministry, you may subscribe to the *The Morning Star Journal*. This bi-monthly periodical contains the latest teachings from **Rick Joyner, Francis Frangipane, Dudley Hall** and others who we feel have a message that is "meat in due season" for the church.

The *Journal* comes in a high quality, large, paperback book form ranging from 64 to 96 pages in length. There are sections for **TEACHING, PROPHECY, INTERCESSION, WORSHIP, BASIC** and **ADVANCED BIBLE STUDIES** as well as a **DIRECTORY** of churches, bookstores, and Christian Professionals. To subscribe send $10.00 for one year's subscription ($20.00 for orders outside the US) to:

The Morning Star Journal
P.O. Box 369
Pineville, NC. 28134

There Were Two Trees In The Garden

by Rick Joyner

This book has been called one of the most significant books to appear in recent times by major Christian leaders. This book goes to the root of each of the trees which have set the course of Christianity — *The Tree of Knowledge of Good and Evil* and *The Tree of Life* as they represent the profound issues of Law and Grace and the nature of True Christianity.

Paperback, 136 pages, **$5.95.**
Available at your local Christian bookstore or you may order directly from MorningStar (see the order form at the back of this book).

Leadership, Management, and the Five Essentials For Success

by Rick Joyner

Leadership is possibly the greatest power entrusted to mere men. We will either use it or be used by it. What is it? How does one get it?

Management is distinguished from *Leadership.* Few true leaders have good management ability, but they will not succeed without it. What is it? How does one get it?

The Five Essentials For Success is a practical, effective management strategy developed to aid effective leaders in becoming effective managers. These applications will work in anything from a household, a church to the largest corporation.

Paperback, 143 pages. **$5.95.**
Available at your local bookstore or you may order directly from MorningStar (see the order form at the back of this book).

REALITY:
The Hope of Glory

by Aaron Katz

"This book is a gripping wake-up call to the church. Of the multitude of books I have read, few have impacted my life as this one has."
— *RICK JOYNER*

Paperback, 156 pages. **$5.95.**
Available at your local Christian bookstore or you may order directly from MorningStar (There is an order form at the back of this book).

Order Form

_____
Name

_____
Address

_____
City, State, Zip

_____
Daytime Phone #

_____ *The Harvest* @ $5.95 ea.

_____ *There Were Two Trees in the Garden* @ $5.95 ea.

_____ *Reality: The Hope of Glory* @ $5.95 ea.

_____ *Leadership, Management and the Five Essentials
For Success* @ $5.95 ea.

_____ 1 Year Subscription to *The Morning Star Journal*
@ $10.00 ($20.00 Outside US)

_____ 1 Year Subscription to The Morning Star "Tape of the
Month" @ $49.00 ($69.00 Outside US)

_____ Shipping & Handling (see chart below)

TOTAL ENCLOSED _____

SEND TO:
MorningStar Publications, P.O. Box 369, Pineville, NC 28134

US Shipping Rates	
< 10.00	1.50
10.00–24.99	2.50
25.00–49.99	3.50
50.00–74.99	4.50
75.00–99.99	5.50
100.00–499.99	6% of total
500.00–999.99	5% of total
> 1,000.00	4% of total

International Shipping Rates	
< 10.00	2.50
10.00–24.99	4.75
25.00–49.99	7.00
50.00–74.99	9.25
75.00–99.99	11.50
100.00–499.99	11% of total
> 500.00	10% of total

* Prices are subject to change without notice. You may request a catalog
with current prices from the above address.